THE COMPLETE GUIDE TO
TITANIC

Sandy Creek
NEW YORK

An Imprint of Sterling Publishing
1166 Avenue of The Americas
New York, NY, 10036

THE COMPLETE GUIDE TO
TITANIC

JULIA GARSTECKI

Sandy Creek
NEW YORK

CONTENTS

DID YOU KNOW?

Words in **bold** are explained in the Glossary on page 140

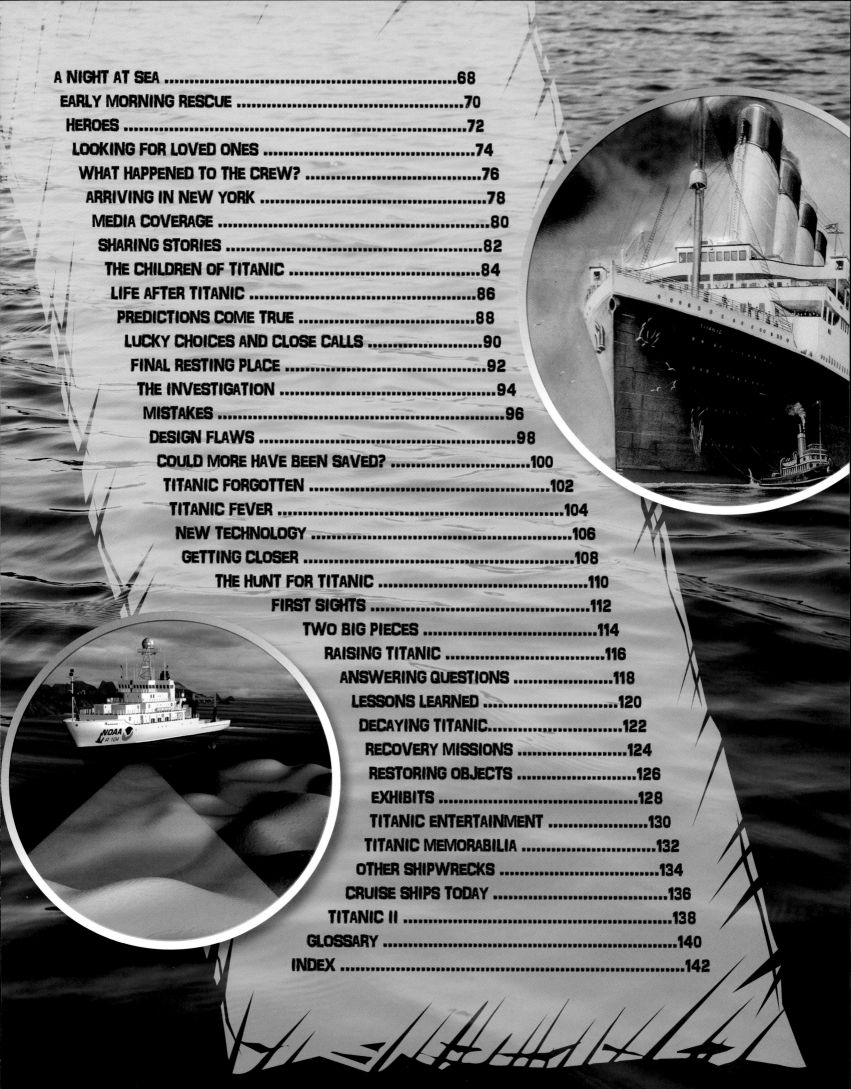

INTRODUCTION

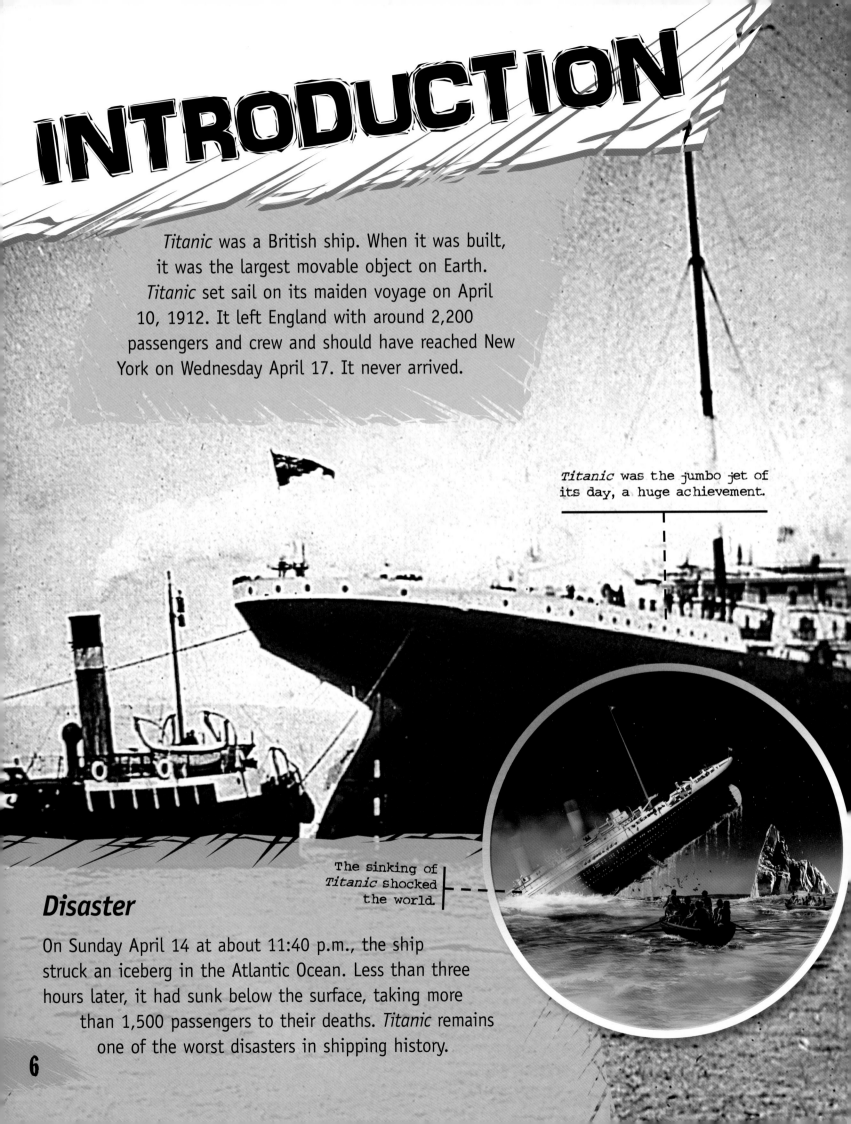

Titanic was a British ship. When it was built, it was the largest movable object on Earth. *Titanic* set sail on its maiden voyage on April 10, 1912. It left England with around 2,200 passengers and crew and should have reached New York on Wednesday April 17. It never arrived.

Titanic was the jumbo jet of its day, a huge achievement.

The sinking of *Titanic* shocked the world.

Disaster

On Sunday April 14 at about 11:40 p.m., the ship struck an iceberg in the Atlantic Ocean. Less than three hours later, it had sunk below the surface, taking more than 1,500 passengers to their deaths. *Titanic* remains one of the worst disasters in shipping history.

Unsinkable?

The White Star Line, the company which owned *Titanic,* called the ship "practically unsinkable"— a very bold claim.

Titanic set off from the docks in Southampton, UK.

DID YOU KNOW?

In *Titanic's* time, wrecks were common. One ship in every hundred sank in the course of one year.

Modern Myth

Titanic's sinking has fascinated people for more than a century. What made the ship sink? Could more people have survived? Who was to blame? It has become a modern myth, and the subject of many books, movies, and TV programs.

CHANGING TRAVEL

Mail, people, and goods were carried by "packet ships."

Ocean travel between Europe and the United States became very popular in the early 20th century. For wealthy people, it was a fun vacation. For the poor, it was the chance to build a new life in America.

Across the Atlantic

Before steam engines were used to power ships in the 19th century, sailing across the Atlantic Ocean took more than six weeks. Ships rocked violently in heavy seas. Most passengers were housed below deck without fresh air. Many became sick and some died during the long crossings.

Life below deck was grim on early Atlantic crossings.

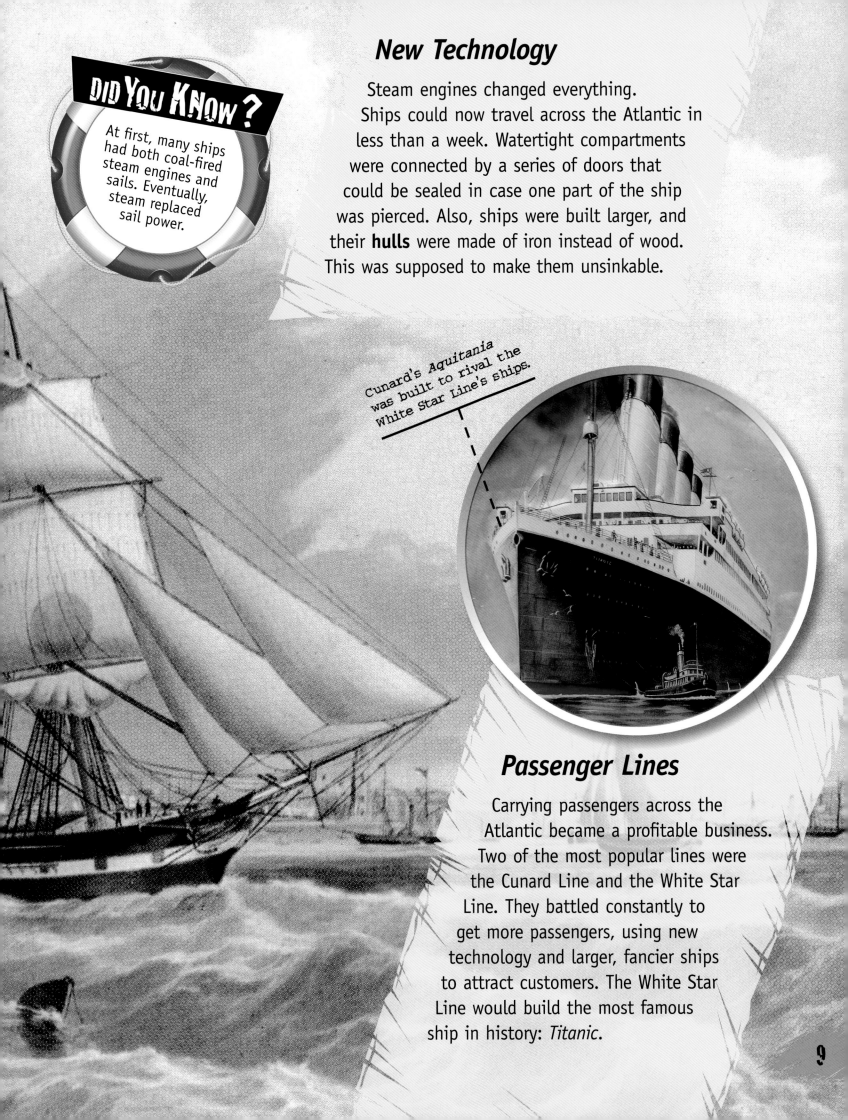

New Technology

Steam engines changed everything.
Ships could now travel across the Atlantic in
less than a week. Watertight compartments
were connected by a series of doors that
could be sealed in case one part of the ship
was pierced. Also, ships were built larger, and
their **hulls** were made of iron instead of wood.
This was supposed to make them unsinkable.

Cunard's *Aquitania*
was built to rival the
White Star Line's ships.

Passenger Lines

Carrying passengers across the
Atlantic became a profitable business.
Two of the most popular lines were
the Cunard Line and the White Star
Line. They battled constantly to
get more passengers, using new
technology and larger, fancier ships
to attract customers. The White Star
Line would build the most famous
ship in history: *Titanic*.

TITANIC TEAM

Harland and Wolff was the world's largest shipyard.

The owner of *Titanic* was J.P. Morgan, an American millionaire. His shipping business, the International Mercantile Marine Co., paid for the ship. Building the huge ship took a talented team of engineers and sailors as well as a lot of money.

J. Bruce Ismay

Ismay was chairman of the International Mercantile Marine Co., which owned the White Star Line. Ismay's goal was to ensure the White Star Line would own the biggest and best ships the world had ever seen.

Ismay survived the *Titanic* disaster.

Lord William Pirrie

Born in Canada, William Pirrie worked his way up from **draftsman** to become the chairman of the Harland and Wolff shipyard in Northern Ireland, where *Titanic* was built. He became the Lord Mayor of Belfast in 1896.

Andrews was the head
naval architect.

Alexander Carlisle and Thomas Andrews

Alexander Carlisle and Thomas Andrews were the lead designers of *Titanic*. It was their job to make sure the ship was exactly what Ismay and Pirrie wanted. Carlisle retired before the ship was completed but Andrews was on board as a first class passenger for the **maiden voyage**.

Captain Edward J. Smith

Captain Smith had commanded many ships before becoming captain of *Titanic* in 1912. He was well liked by his crew and passengers, and had intended to retire after returning to England. He was last seen going into *Titanic's* wheelhouse before the ship sank.

DID YOU KNOW?

Titanic's owner, J.P. Morgan wasn't on board the ship on its maiden voyage because he was ill. This illness saved his life.

11

A DREAM IS BORN

Before *Titanic* could be built, a team of expert designers drew the ship's plans. The goal was to create a luxury ship—a giant floating hotel with the best food, drink, and facilities—that would appeal to the wealthiest passengers.

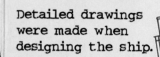

Detailed drawings were made when designing the ship.

SHELTER DECK C
SALOON DECK D
UPPER DECK E
MIDDLE DECK F
LOWER DECK G

Designing the Ship

William Pirrie personally oversaw the draftsmen who made the first drawings of *Titanic*. Then it was the job of the designers Alexander Carlisle, and later Thomas Andrews, to turn the grand ideas into reality.

Pirrie did not sail on *Titanic*. He died later in 1924.

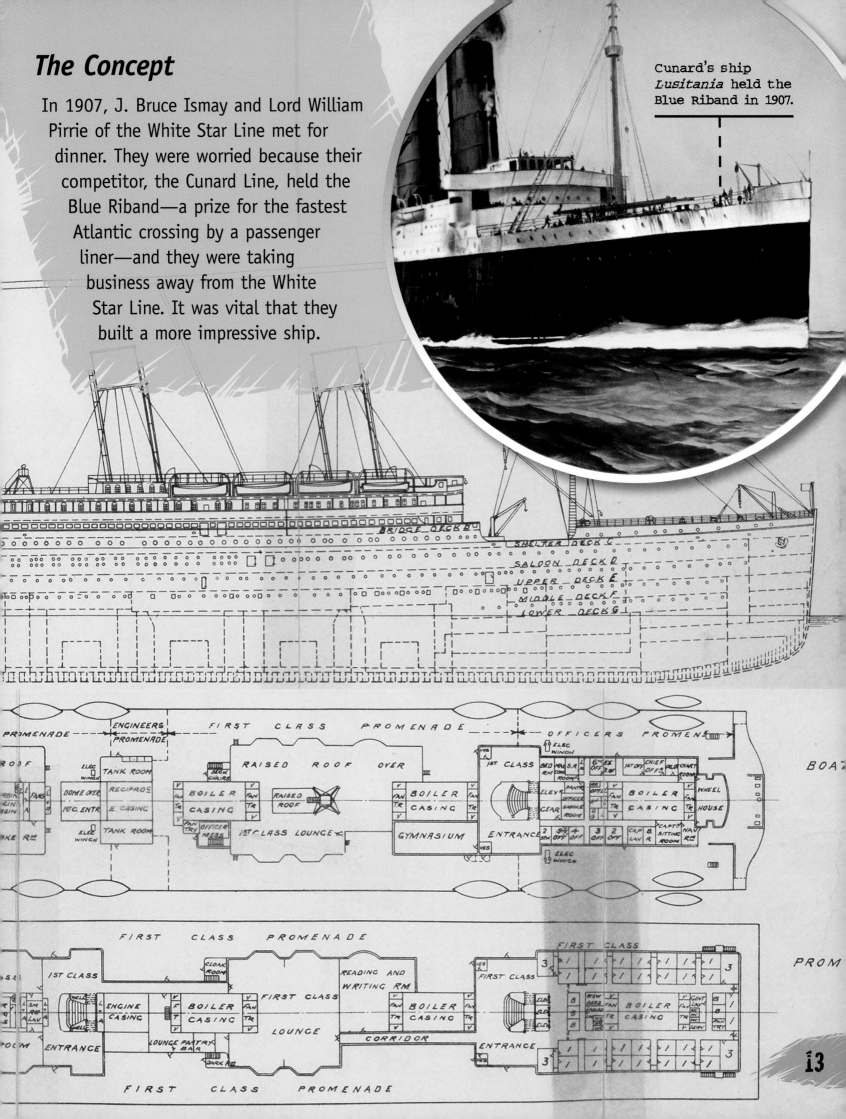

The Concept

In 1907, J. Bruce Ismay and Lord William Pirrie of the White Star Line met for dinner. They were worried because their competitor, the Cunard Line, held the Blue Riband—a prize for the fastest Atlantic crossing by a passenger liner—and they were taking business away from the White Star Line. It was vital that they built a more impressive ship.

Cunard's ship *Lusitania* held the Blue Riband in 1907.

BRIDGE DECK B
SHELTER DECK C
SALOON DECK D
UPPER DECK E
MIDDLE DECK F
LOWER DECK G

PROMENADE
ENGINEERS PROMENADE
FIRST CLASS PROMENADE
OFFICERS PROMEN
BOAT

ROOF
ELEC WINCH
TANK ROOM
RAISED ROOF OVER
1ST CLASS
ELEC WINCH
BED RM
M.S.R. COM ROOM
6'X EX OFF
1ST OFF
CHIEF OFFS
PILOT CHART ROOM

DOME OVER
RECIPROS
DECK CHAIRS
BOILER CASING
FAN TR
RAISED ROOF
FAN TR
BOILER CASING
FAN TR
OFFICERS
ELEV
PANTRY
STATE ROOM
BOILER CASING
TR
WHEEL HOUSE

ELEC ENTR
E CASING
FAN TRY OFFICER MESS
1ST CLASS LOUNGE
GYMNASIUM
ENTRANCE
GEAR
SMOKE ROOM
2 STW OFF
5'X OFF
4 OFF
3 OFF
2 OFF
CAP & LAV R
CAPT'S SITTING ROOM
NAV ROOM

ELEC WINCH
TANK ROOM
ELEC WINCH

FIRST CLASS PROMENADE
FIRST CLASS
PROM

1ST CLASS
CLOAK ROOM
READING AND WRITING RM
1ST CLASS
FIRST CLASS
3
3

SM LAV
ENGINE CASING
BOILER CASING
FAN TR
FIRST CLASS
FAN TR
BOILER CASING
FAN TR
BOILER CASING
FAN TR

ENTRANCE
LOUNGE PANTRY & BAR
DARK RM
LOUNGE
CORRIDOR
ENTRANCE

FIRST CLASS PROMENADE

BUILDING THE SHIP

When it was first floated, or **launched**, in 1911, *Titanic* was the largest movable object on Earth. Building the ship was an impressive feat but it is sadly best known as the most famous shipwreck in history.

Funnels let smoke and steam escape from the engine room.

DID YOU KNOW?

Three million rivets were used on *Titanic* to hold the giant steel plates of the hull together.

Preparing to Build

Construction of *Titanic* began on March 31, 1909. Both *Titanic* and its sister ship, *Olympic*, were built in Belfast, Northern Ireland. Before work on building the 883-foot ship started, a giant frame 200 feet tall was assembled. This held the ship's hull. Sixteen moveable cranes were needed to move supplies around.

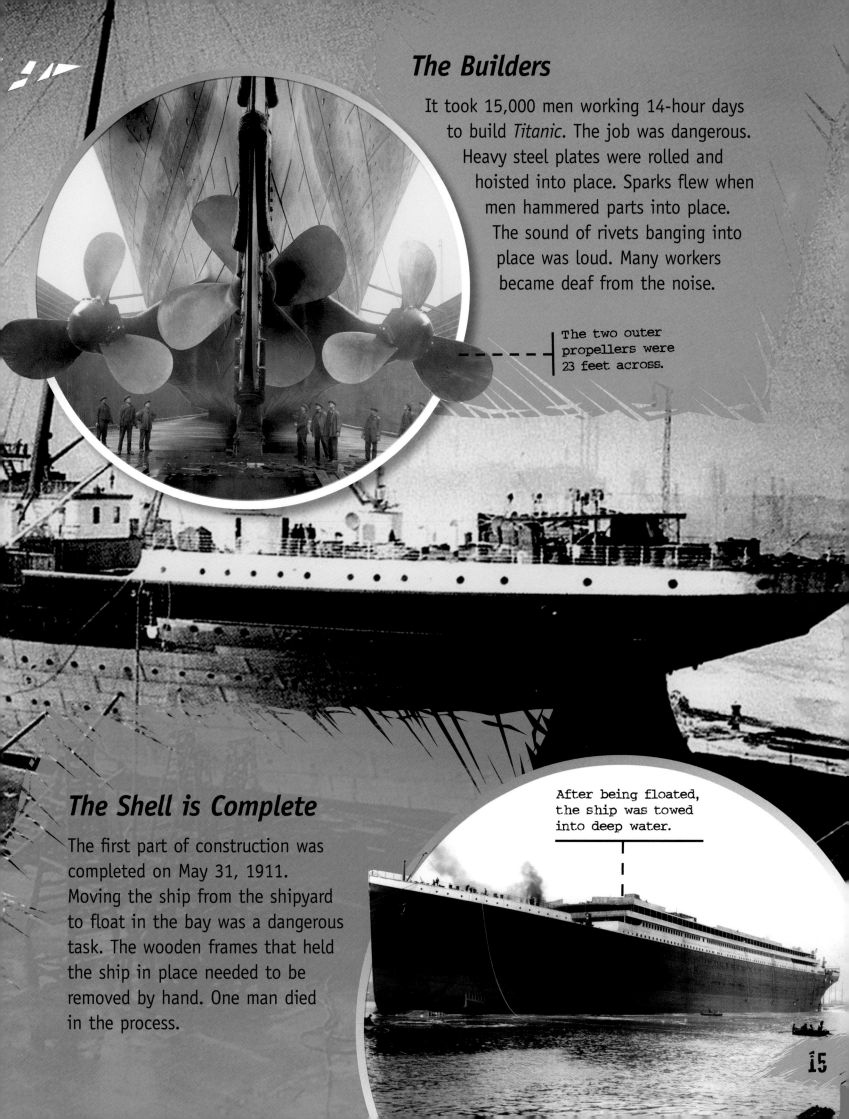

The Builders

It took 15,000 men working 14-hour days to build *Titanic*. The job was dangerous. Heavy steel plates were rolled and hoisted into place. Sparks flew when men hammered parts into place. The sound of rivets banging into place was loud. Many workers became deaf from the noise.

The two outer propellers were 23 feet across.

The Shell is Complete

The first part of construction was completed on May 31, 1911. Moving the ship from the shipyard to float in the bay was a dangerous task. The wooden frames that held the ship in place needed to be removed by hand. One man died in the process.

After being floated, the ship was towed into deep water.

COMPLETING TITANIC

After *Titanic* was floated in May 1911, it needed to be finished, or fitted out. Work began to install engines, propellers, and other engineering components, as well as the cabins and passenger facilities.

One of *Titanic's* giant engines is prepared for fitting.

Funnels and Engines

On May 31, 1911, the shell of *Titanic* was launched into the River Lagan. It was anchored in deep water while mechanical equipment, including engines and boilers, were put in place. The four funnels were hoisted into position, as were chandeliers, decorative wood paneling, stained glass windows, and plush carpets.

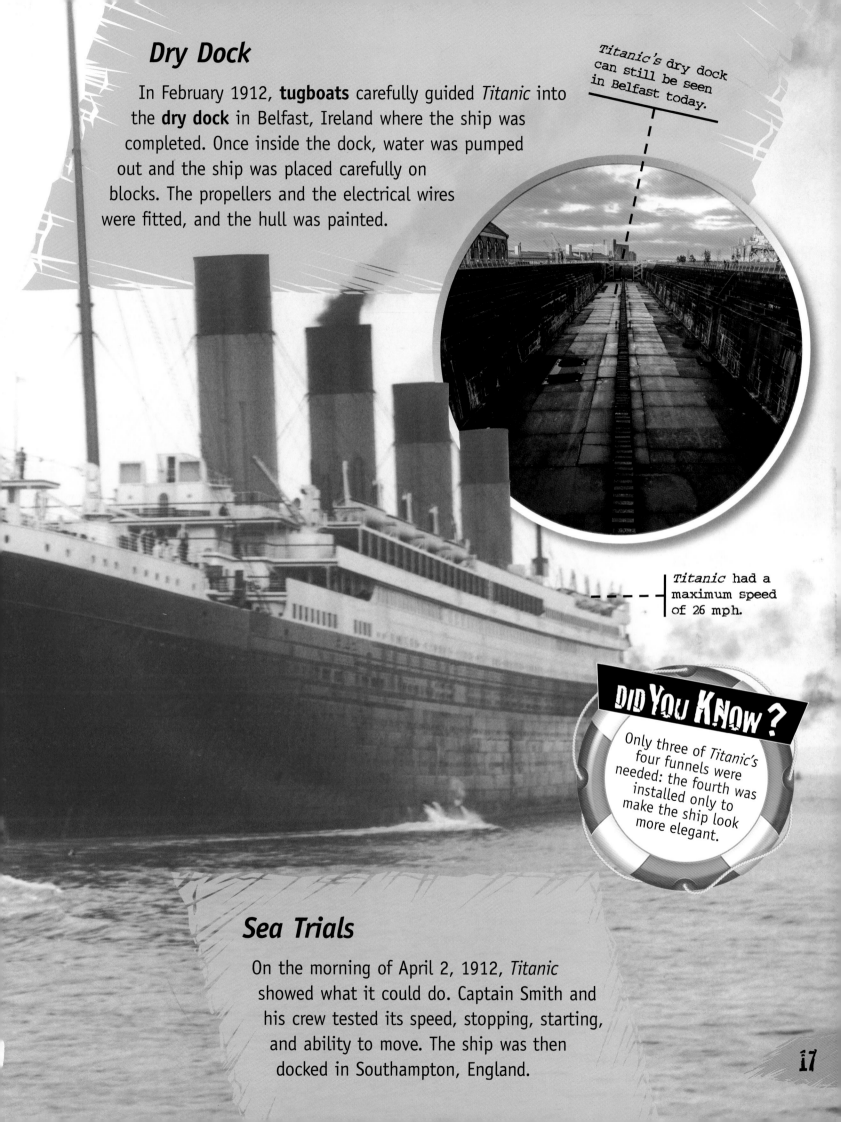

Dry Dock

In February 1912, **tugboats** carefully guided *Titanic* into the **dry dock** in Belfast, Ireland where the ship was completed. Once inside the dock, water was pumped out and the ship was placed carefully on blocks. The propellers and the electrical wires were fitted, and the hull was painted.

Titanic's dry dock can still be seen in Belfast today.

Titanic had a maximum speed of 26 mph.

DID YOU KNOW?

Only three of *Titanic's* four funnels were needed: the fourth was installed only to make the ship look more elegant.

Sea Trials

On the morning of April 2, 1912, *Titanic* showed what it could do. Captain Smith and his crew tested its speed, stopping, starting, and ability to move. The ship was then docked in Southampton, England.

TECHNOLOGY AT SEA

Titanic was fitted with the latest technology of the day. Its radio and electrical systems were state-of-the-art. Some cabins even had telephones so people could make calls to others on the ship.

DID YOU KNOW?

In 1912, long-distance **wireless** was a new technology. It was invented by the Italian engineer Gugliemo Marconi.

Electrical Control Panel

The ship's electrical systems, such as its lighting, fans, and generators, were managed through a central control panel. This also regulated the equipment that turned steam into water and removed salt from sea water to make it drinkable.

Wireless

The invention of long-range wireless meant ships were no longer alone after they left port. *Titanic's* transmitter could send messages in Morse code over distances of up to 2,000 miles. When *Titanic* began to sink, the wireless operators looked for help by **telegraphing** other ships.

Rivets were used to make ships, bridges, and engines.

The Hull

The hull of *Titanic* was made of steel plates. Some were more than 6 feet tall, 36 feet long, and one inch thick. Over 24,000 tons of steel were used for the hull, and 1,500 tons of steel were used in the **rivets**. The anchors and anchor chains were also made of steel. Each individual link in the anchor chain weighed 175 pounds—as much as a person.

There were two wireless operators aboard *Titanic*.

Titanic had three huge steel anchors.

19

SISTER SHIPS

Titanic was one of three "sister" ships built for the White Star Line. They all had four funnels, and were driven by three propellers, but were slightly different in size and in internal features.

Olympic was the only one of the sisters not to sink.

Olympic

The first of the sisters to be built was *Olympic*. Like *Titanic*, it was named after a group of gods from Ancient Greek mythology. *Olympic* was just as beautiful as *Titanic*, but slightly smaller. *Olympic* was used to carry soldiers in World War I and even rammed and sank a German submarine. It was scrapped in 1936.

Olympic and *Titanic* were built at the Harland and Wolff shipyard in Belfast.

Titanic was built next to its smaller sister Olympic.

Britannic

The third of the sister ships was originally going to be named Gigantic, but its name was changed because it sounded too similar to Titanic. Built after Titanic, with added safety features, it became a hospital ship in World War I. In November 1916, the ship struck a mine and sank.

On board Britannic when it sank were 1,066 medical staff, crew, and soldiers.

POWERING TITANIC

Titanic's passengers never saw the engineering that powered the world's largest ship across the Atlantic Ocean. The engines could deliver about 50,000 **horsepower**, which was a large amount at the time, but less than a single modern airliner engine.

Older Technolgy

Titanic's competitors, the Cunard Line, had access to newer technology for their engines. Titanic's old-fashioned engines were enough to drive the ship to a top speed of 24 **knots**, some two knots slower than Cunard's fastest vessels.

Boilers

The ship had 29 **boilers**. They were fueled by more than 800 tons of coal each day. Men called trimmers brought coal to the firemen, who put the coal in the boilers to heat water and produce steam. The steam powered the ship's engines.

Each of the funnels was wider than a steam train.

Engines

Titanic was powered by two **steam engines**—the largest that existed at the time—and one smaller **turbine**. The energy of the steam turned the mighty propellers. Then, the steam ran into a condenser and was turned back into water. This was pumped back to the boilers to be heated again.

About 150 men worked in *Titanic's* boiler room.

23

JOBS ON BOARD

Thousands of people helped create, build, and maintain *Titanic* both on land and at sea. In Southampton, England, people queued up to apply for jobs aboard the prestigious liner.

Workers leave the shipyard at the end of a day.

Building the Ship

About 15,000 men worked on the construction of the ship. Steel workers, cabinet makers, plumbers, and painters were hired to complete the massive project, and many brought their families with them. Skilled workers were paid £2, or around $10, per week, while unskilled laborers earned half that amount.

Crew carried the luggage for first class passengers.

DID YOU KNOW?

Titanic had 69 chefs, bakers, and dish-washers working in its kitchens.

There were more than 300 stewards on board *Titanic*.

On Board

Once *Titanic* set sail, a huge crew was needed to keep it running smoothly. There were officers, deck crew, engineers, firemen, and electricians. Most of those workers were never seen by passengers. There were also cooks, laundry staff to wash sheets and towels, waiters, postal clerks, and stewards who made sure guests had everything they needed.

THE PLANNED VOYAGE

Titanic attracted a big audience everywhere it sailed. Its launch in Belfast was attended by thousands of people. Thousands planned to greet the ship in New York City when it arrived.

The docks were crowded as people boarded the ship.

Collecting Passengers

On Wednesday, April 3, 1912, *Titanic* left Belfast and arrived in Southampton, England. Here, final arrangements were made, including taking on more crew for the journey. The first passengers boarded, and the ship then sailed to Cherbourg, France, to drop off and pick up more people. Hours later, it sailed to Queenstown, Ireland, to pick up its final passengers.

Passengers were picked up from several places.

Belfast 1

IRELAND

Queenstown (Cork) 4

GREAT BRITAIN

Southampton 2

3 Cherbourg

FRANCE

Titanic sank more than 500 miles from New York.

Belfast

4 Cork

USA New York

Titanic hits iceberg

DID YOU KNOW?

2,220 people were aboard *Titanic* on her maiden voyage, including at least 13 couples on their honeymoon.

Heading into the Ocean

On Thursday, April 11, *Titanic* left Queenstown and headed out into the Atlantic Ocean. She logged about 386 miles between Thursday and Friday. On Saturday and Sunday, the ship traveled a further 1,000 miles. The ship was due in New York on Wednesday, April 17, but its captain hoped to arrive early, on Tuesday, April 16, to impress the world.

PREPARING TO SAIL

The scene at the docks in Southampton before *Titanic* set sail was one of whirling activity. Fuel, cargo, and provisions were loaded and a lifeboat drill was carried out before the passengers embarked.

Fuel Shortage

Crossing the Atlantic Ocean required thousands of tons of coal. There was a coal-miners' strike when *Titanic* was preparing for travel. This meant that the White Star Line could not get coal for the ship. To solve this problem, the White Star Line docked their other ships. Then, they took coal from those ships and loaded it onto *Titanic*.

Coal was loaded on to the ship's Orlop Deck.

Stocking the Ship

It would take a lot of food to prepare meals for over 2,200 people during the week-long voyage. The ship was stocked with about 80,000 pounds of fresh sausage, beef, chicken, and fish. Thousands of pounds of fruit and vegetables were loaded along with baking ingredients and ice cream. *Titanic* carried more than 3,000 bottles of champagne, 15,000 bottles of beer, and 8,000 cigars.

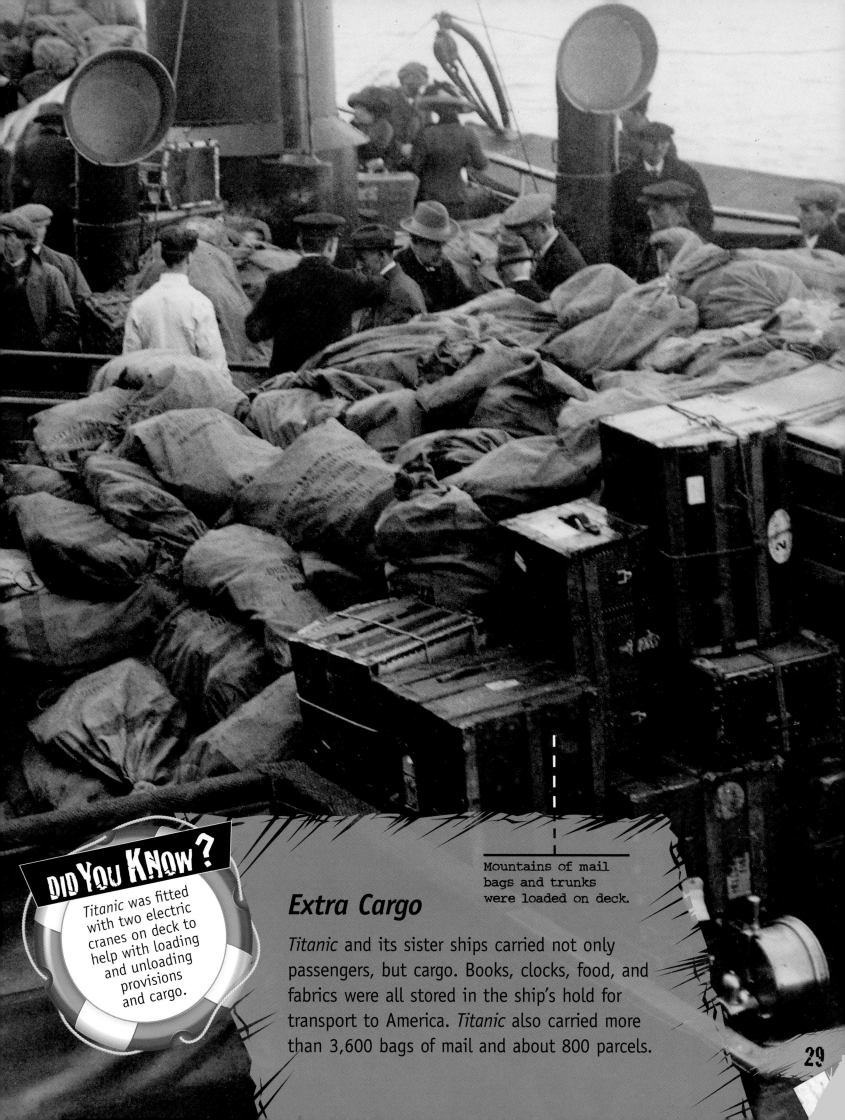

Mountains of mail bags and trunks were loaded on deck.

Extra Cargo

Titanic and its sister ships carried not only passengers, but cargo. Books, clocks, food, and fabrics were all stored in the ship's hold for transport to America. *Titanic* also carried more than 3,600 bags of mail and about 800 parcels.

29

EARLY PROBLEMS

With the crew and passengers in high spirits, *Titanic* set sail on her maiden voyage from Southampton, England, at noon on Wednesday April 10, 1912. However, the ship was about to face some problems early in its voyage.

The liner *New York* almost hit *Titanic* in the docks.

DID YOU KNOW?

Titanic was too big to dock at the French port of Cherbourg, so passengers were ferried out in smaller boats.

A Close Call

As *Titanic* was leaving Southampton, it passed close by the moored ship *New York*. A big wave made *New York* break free and head straight for *Titanic*. Only quick thinking from Captain Smith and the action of a nearby tug kept the two ships from colliding.

Fire on Board

Coal was loaded on to *Titanic* from other ships owned by the White Star Line. As the coal was taken on, a fire started in the starboard bunker of Boiler Room 6. Twelve men were in charge of putting the fire out. The fire was kept secret from passengers and reporters. It continued to smolder until April 13th, well after the ship left the dock.

The smoldering coal was fed into the ship's boilers.

Wireless Breakdown

Passengers could send and receive telegrams from the *Titanic* for a small fee, but on Friday, the wireless device broke down. The operators worked hard to repair the equipment so that passengers would not get upset. In between many messages to and from friends and family, reports about ice in the Atlantic were starting to come in.

Messages were tapped out in Morse code using a key.

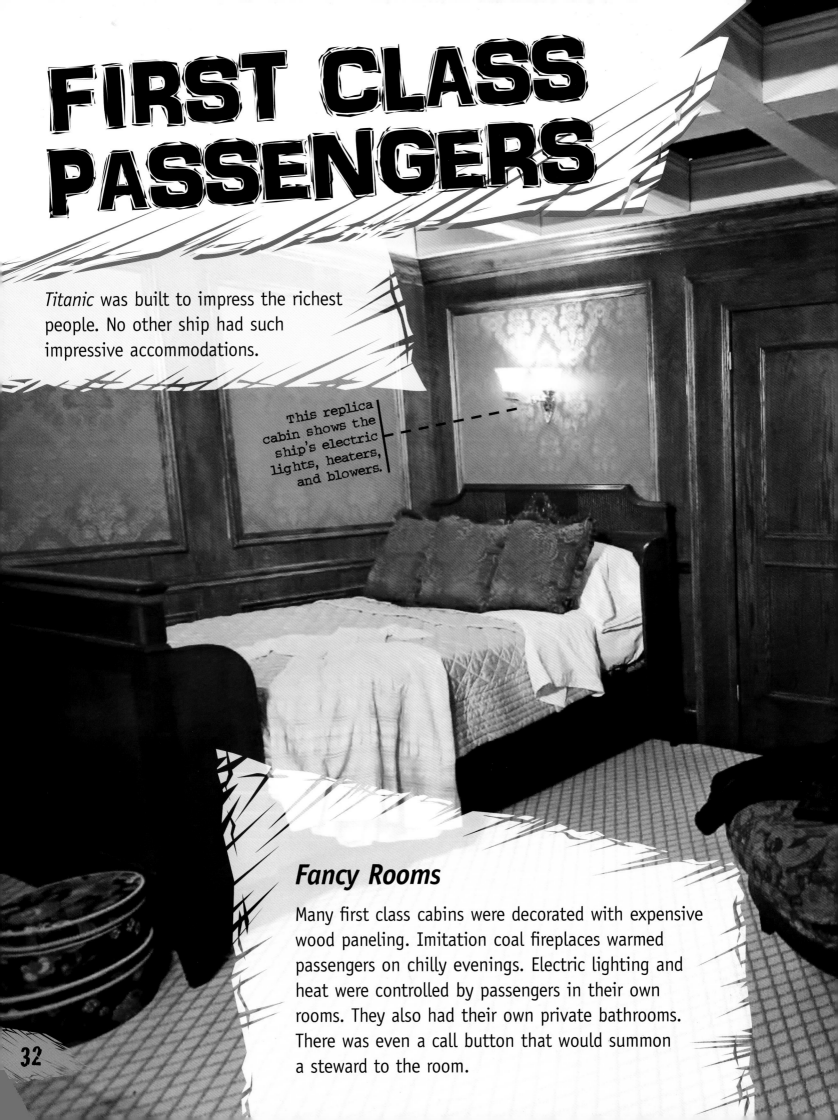

FIRST CLASS PASSENGERS

Titanic was built to impress the richest people. No other ship had such impressive accommodations.

This replica cabin shows the ship's electric lights, heaters, and blowers.

Fancy Rooms

Many first class cabins were decorated with expensive wood paneling. Imitation coal fireplaces warmed passengers on chilly evenings. Electric lighting and heat were controlled by passengers in their own rooms. They also had their own private bathrooms. There was even a call button that would summon a steward to the room.

Wealthy Passengers

Most ships sailing across the Atlantic made their money from poorer people moving to America. *Titanic* was different, focusing on the wealthy. The average first class room cost £300, or $1,500.00. That was a lot of money in 1912. The grandest rooms were £870 pounds, or $4,300.

Passengers included aristocrats such as Lady Duff Gordon.

First Class Survivors

The first class passengers had the highest rates of survival. About 97 percent of female first class passengers survived the sinking. Women and children were given the first opportunities to board the lifeboats.

Almost all children in first and second class survived.

DID YOU KNOW?

First class suites were decorated in different styles. The wealthiest passengers could request which room they preferred.

SECOND CLASS PASSENGERS

There were about 300 second class passengers aboard *Titanic*. They were not entitled to everything the first class passengers enjoyed. However, traveling second class on *Titanic* was very similar to traveling first class on smaller ships.

The Passengers

Most of the second class passengers were tourists. They included teachers, religious leaders, and musicians. It cost about £12, or $60, for the trip. The cabins had bunk-beds and were fitted with sinks and mirrors, although passengers had to share toilets.

Second class rooms had a small couch and writing desk.

Activities Aboard

There were many things for second class passengers to do. They had a Promenade Deck, where they could walk and enjoy the fresh air. A library offered reading materials for both adults and children. Men spent time in the smoking room as well.

Passengers could stroll and socialize on the deck.

DID YOU KNOW?

The Second Class promenade was in the aft, or rear, of the ship. It was lit at night by electric lamps.

Survival Rates

All the children and around 86 percent of the women in second class survived the sinking. Unfortunately, only about 8 percent of men traveling in second class survived.

Survivors gather on the deck of a rescue ship.

35

THIRD CLASS PASSENGERS

Emigrants seeking a better life in the United States made up the majority of third class passengers crossing the Atlantic at this time. There were about 700 on *Titanic*. They came from all over the world, but most were from Ireland, Sweden, Russia, and Finland.

Ready for a Better Life

Emigrants saved up for a long time to buy their third class tickets, which cost around £5, or about $25. They brought all their belongings with them to start a new life in America. Many passengers were mothers with their children, sailing to join their husbands who already had work in America.

Accommodations

The accommodation may have been third class, but it was far better than on other ships, and often better than people's own homes. People slept four to a cabin. They had running water and electricity. Toilets and bathtubs were shared.

Men relaxed in the third class smoking room.

Dining and Entertainment

Third class passengers on other ships usually had to bring their own food on board. On *Titanic*, however, hot meals were provided. People ate seated at long tables. They were not allowed in the pool or gym with the first class passengers, but they had areas to play games and talk.

Third class cabins were cozy but comfortable.

Survival

Only 25 percent of third class passengers survived the *Titanic* disaster. There were many reasons for this. They were furthest from the lifeboats; some gates that separated third class from other areas of the ship were locked. Many spoke poor English so could not understand the crew.

Rhoda "Rosa" Abbott survived after being pulled from the sea.

FAMOUS PASSENGERS

Titanic attracted many wealthy passengers. Some were well-known and enjoyed the best accommodations. Many passengers who were not famous before the voyage became famous later simply for having been on *Titanic*.

Dorothy Gibson

Dorothy Gibson was a model and film star. After making many movies, she decided to go to Europe for a vacation. A movie she was working on needed her to come home early. She boarded *Titanic* and survived the disaster. Soon after, she starred in the movie *Saved From the Titanic*. She played herself and re-enacted her trip.

Dorothy Gibson escaped on the first lifeboat launched.

Molly Brown

Molly Brown's real name was Margaret Tobin. She grew up in the southern United States. She worked to improve human rights and dedicated her life to helping others. She was traveling in Europe and decided to come home early and boarded *Titanic*.

Molly Brown helped raise money for *Titanic* survivors.

John Jacob Astor IV

John Jacob Astor IV was one of the first American multi-millionaires. He was well known for many things. He wrote a book, developed a bicycle brake, and built the Astoria Hotel, a famous hotel in New York City.

Astor did not survive the *Titanic* disaster.

EXPLORING THE DECKS

Titanic was designed to carry 3,385 people, including about 960 crew. The ship had ten decks, connected by stairs and—for the first class passengers—elevators. Each deck had its special uses.

DID YOU KNOW?

The front of a ship is referred to as "fore"; the back of the ship, or the stern, is referred to as "aft".

First class passengers could sit on a spacious deck.

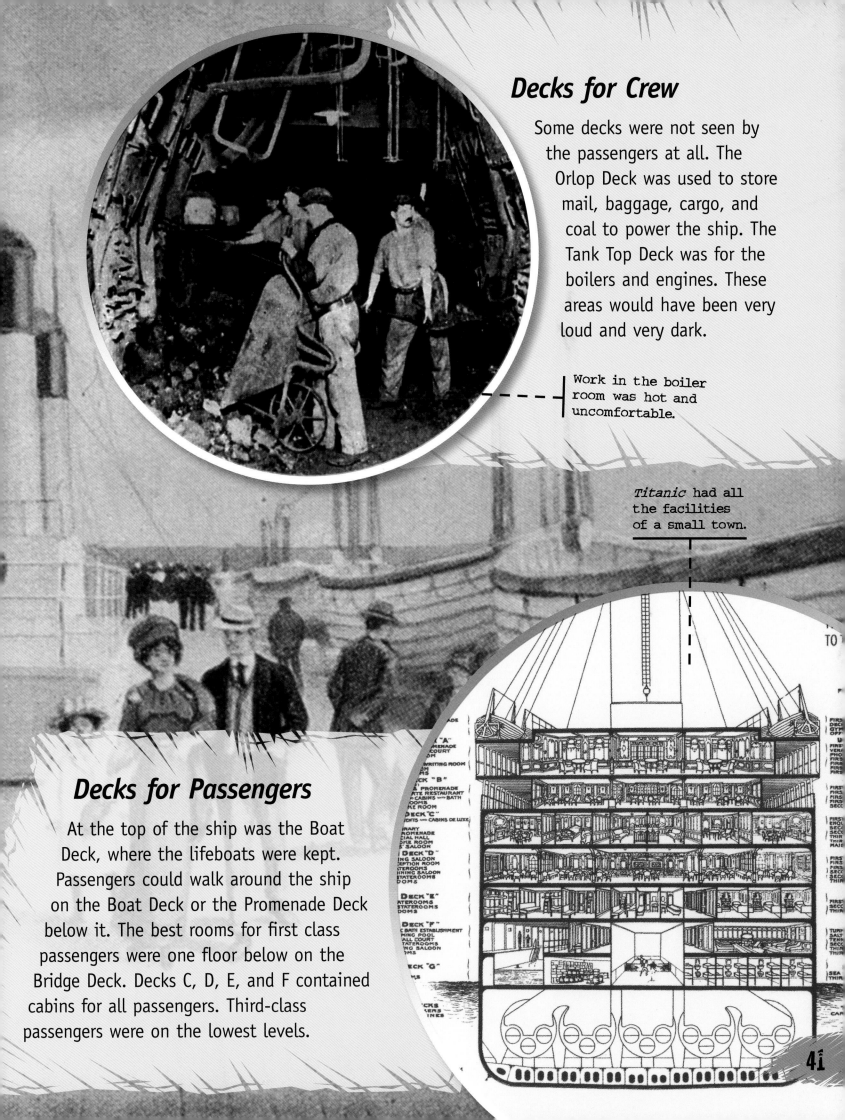

Decks for Crew

Some decks were not seen by the passengers at all. The Orlop Deck was used to store mail, baggage, cargo, and coal to power the ship. The Tank Top Deck was for the boilers and engines. These areas would have been very loud and very dark.

Work in the boiler room was hot and uncomfortable.

Titanic had all the facilities of a small town.

Decks for Passengers

At the top of the ship was the Boat Deck, where the lifeboats were kept. Passengers could walk around the ship on the Boat Deck or the Promenade Deck below it. The best rooms for first class passengers were one floor below on the Bridge Deck. Decks C, D, E, and F contained cabins for all passengers. Third-class passengers were on the lowest levels.

ANIMALS ABOARD

Titanic wasn't just carrying humans—there were animal passengers on board too! Dogs, cats, and roosters were known to be on the vessel, and were cared for by the crew of the ship. There was even a dog show planned for later in the voyage, but of course it never happened.

Crew members took the dogs for walks on deck.

DID YOU KNOW?

A pig was rescued from *Titanic*—but not a real one! It was a pig-shaped music box owned by Edith Rosenbaum.

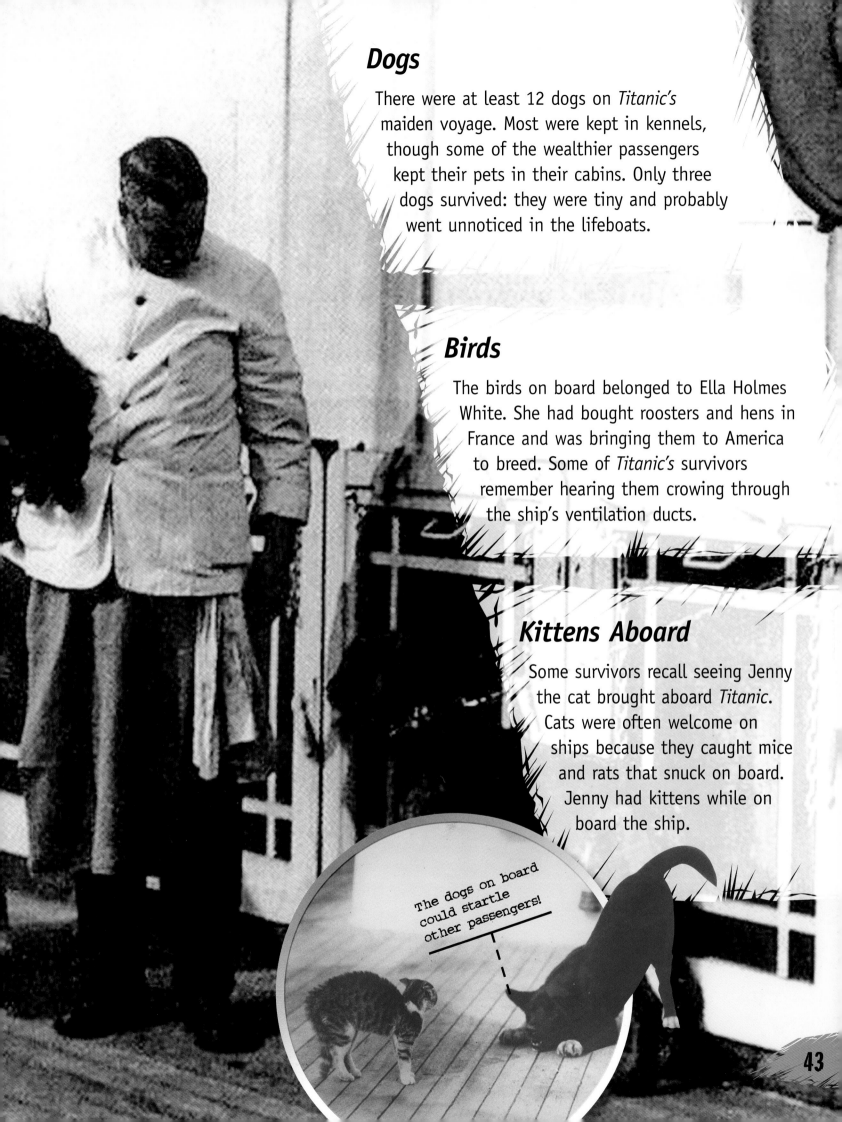

Dogs

There were at least 12 dogs on *Titanic's* maiden voyage. Most were kept in kennels, though some of the wealthier passengers kept their pets in their cabins. Only three dogs survived: they were tiny and probably went unnoticed in the lifeboats.

Birds

The birds on board belonged to Ella Holmes White. She had bought roosters and hens in France and was bringing them to America to breed. Some of *Titanic's* survivors remember hearing them crowing through the ship's ventilation ducts.

Kittens Aboard

Some survivors recall seeing Jenny the cat brought aboard *Titanic*. Cats were often welcome on ships because they caught mice and rats that snuck on board. Jenny had kittens while on board the ship.

The dogs on board could startle other passengers!

43

STAYING HEALTHY

Titanic was built to attract the wealthiest passengers, so there were many things to do on board, especially in first class. Privileged passengers could swim in a pool, play squash and other games, and use the gymnasium and the Turkish baths.

The Swimming Pool

The heated swimming pool was only the second of its kind on a ship. The first was on *Titanic's* sister ship, *Olympic*. Seawater from the ocean was pumped in to fill it. Showers were available to rinse the saltwater off after a swim.

The water in *Titanic's* pool was heated for comfort.

Rowing in the gym was said to be "good for the liver."

The Gymnasium

There were many things to do in the gym. A trainer was available to help passengers with the stationary bike, rowing machine, or weights. Boxing and other sports were also played in the gym.

Shuffleboard was a popular game for passengers.

Physical Activity for All

Second class passengers also enjoyed playing active games. There was ring toss and shuffleboard. Both second and third class passengers could also stroll along some of the ship's decks.

KEEPING BUSY

There was something for everyone on board *Titanic*.
First and second class passengers could read, or write
letters in the library, and there was even a darkroom
for those interested in the new pastime of photography.

Socializing

People from many different countries
and many professions were aboard
Titanic. There were a lot of places
throughout the ship for people to
meet and talk about world events
or play board games such as chess,
backgammon, and cards.

Music

Two different groups of musicians —a **quintet** and a **trio**—played aboard *Titanic* at different times of the day. They were paid well and enjoyed second class accommodation.

This film still shows third class passengers making their own music.

People could take a stroll or have a nap in one of the deck chairs.

Children played with spinning tops and toys on deck.

Children's Games

Children—especially those in third class—often went off to explore the ship. They sometimes played on cranes in the cargo room, or watched the workers in the boiler room. There were children from many different countries to play with.

ART ON BOARD

There is a myth that *Titanic* was filled with precious paintings by famous artists like Monet and Picasso. There were some impressive works of art on the ship, but none were by such renowned artists. However, many passengers had valuable jewelry.

Ah Moon of my delight who knowest no wane,
The Moon of Heaven is rising once again :
How oft hereafter rising shall she look
Through this same garden after me — in vain.

75

And when Thyself with shining foot shall pass
Among the guests star-scattered on the grass,
And in thy joyous errand reach the spot
Where I made one — turn down an empty glass !

TAMAM SHUD

The *Rubaiyat* is a book of poems by Omar Khayyam.

Books

One of the most famous works lost on *Titanic* was a book of Persian poetry known as the *Rubaiyat*. The book's cover was covered in rubies, emeralds, and amethysts. The book was being carried on *Titanic* to a collector in the United States.

Jewelry

Wealthy passengers brought expensive jewelry with them on their crossing of the Atlantic. Rings and necklaces with precious stones would have been on board. Many of the pieces were recovered and are now part of exhibits about the disaster.

Many passengers carried pocket watches; some were gold or inlaid with gems.

The painter Francis Davis Millet stands in front of one of his murals.

Francis Davis Millet

A big loss to the art world was Francis Davis Millet, who died in the *Titanic* disaster. He was a well-known American painter who had been a drummer boy in the Civil War. He was most famous for painting **murals**.

49

TITANIC MUSICIANS

There were eight musicians on *Titanic's* maiden voyage. Their job was to entertain first and second class passengers. The musicians became heroes when *Titanic* sank because they played music to keep up the spirits of the doomed passengers.

DID YOU KNOW?

As the ship sank, the last song played by the orchestra was probably the hymn, "Nearer, My God, to Thee."

The Orchestra

The eight musicians were divided into two groups—a quintet that played after dinner and during religious services, and a trio of violin, cello, and piano that played in the café and restaurant. This way music could be heard throughout the day.

All the musicians went down with *Titanic*.

The band played for over an hour on the deck of *Titanic*.

Heroes

The two groups of musicians, led by band leader Wallace Hartley, only played together one time when on board. This was when *Titanic* began to sink, and the lifeboats were lowered. Survivors remember seeing passengers in gowns, with their life jackets on, listening to the music on deck. The orchestra played popular tunes such as "Alexander's Ragtime Band" and "In the Shadows." They bravely played on until the angle of the sinking ship was so steep that playing became impossible.

Wallace Hartley was the band's leader and violinist.

51

MEALS ABOARD TITANIC

Titanic's galley (kitchen) prepared about 6,000 meals each day, and the ship's restaurants rivaled the finest dining establishments in London and Paris. The galley included a butcher's shop, a bakery, and vast storage bins for all the coal needed to fuel the ovens.

Kitchen Workers

First and second class passengers enjoyed excellent food aboard—indeed the ship's head chef, Charles Proctor, was one of the highest-paid member of the crew. Meals were served three times a day. If passengers were hungry in between meal times, they could order sandwiches or snacks in a café.

The first class dining room was in the middle of the ship.

Over 60 chefs and many waiters worked on board.

Fine Meals for All

The first class dining room was beautiful and elegant. Dinner could be 13 courses, each with its own matching wine, and last several hours. Second class passengers ate food from the same kitchens, and even third class passengers were well fed with hearty stews, soups, fresh bread, and pudding.

Titanic carried 127,000 pieces of tableware, such as plates.

DID YOU KNOW?

The first class dining room had space for 500 people. A **bugle** was played to announce dinner time.

CALM CONDITIONS

Titanic was built to withstand the often harsh weather conditions of the Atlantic Ocean. But on the night she sank, the weather was calm. The stillness of the sea, the low temperature of the water, and even the position of the Moon could have all contributed to the *Titanic* disaster.

Optical Illusion

Titanic was sailing where the cold waters of the Labrador Current meet the warmer waters of the Gulf Stream. Layers of cold air sink below layers of warm air. This can cause a mirage that makes objects appear higher and closer than they actually are. The area between where an object seems to be and where it actually is can appear hazy. The iceberg that *Titanic* hit may have been hidden in the haze, where it would have been hard to see.

Optical illusions make it difficult to judge distance.

A New Moon

On the night of the *Titanic* disaster, there was only a tiny sliver of Moon visible. There was very little moonlight, which made spotting any obstacles ahead more difficult. The night was calm, which meant there were no large waves to break on an iceberg and give away its position.

The waning Moon was just visible on the night *Titanic* sank.

DID YOU KNOW?

The word "iceberg" is used for pieces of floating ice that are over 16 feet across. Smaller chunks are called "growlers".

High Tide

The Moon may have been responsible for the disaster in an indirect way. When the Moon and Sun are in line, they cause very high tides in the Earth's oceans. Just such an alignment had happened in January 1912. Some scientists think that the resulting high tide brought an exceptional number of icebergs into the North Atlantic in the spring—it was one of these that *Titanic* hit.

There were more icebergs than usual in the ocean.

ICEBERGS

Back in 1912, there was no radar, sonar, or satellite technology to help ships navigate and avoid obstacles. The captain of *Titanic* had to rely on lookouts to spot icebergs and other dangers that lay in the path of the ship.

Ice chunks break off ice sheets into the sea, in a process called "calving."

How an Iceberg is Made

Icebergs start life on land, as fallen snow that is pushed together to make a thick ice shelf, or **glacier**. Large chunks of this ice break off and float in the cold seas and lakes. Any pieces more than 16 feet across are called icebergs.

GREENLAND

West Greenland Current

East Greenland current

Labrador Current

Icy Travelers

The iceberg that sank *Titanic* was created on the coast of Greenland. Ocean currents carried it down the coast of Canada. Another current, called the Gulf Stream, which moves across the Atlantic Ocean then pushed it into the path of *Titanic*.

CANADA

Titanic collision

GULF STREAM

The journey of the iceberg that hit *Titanic* was thousands of miles long.

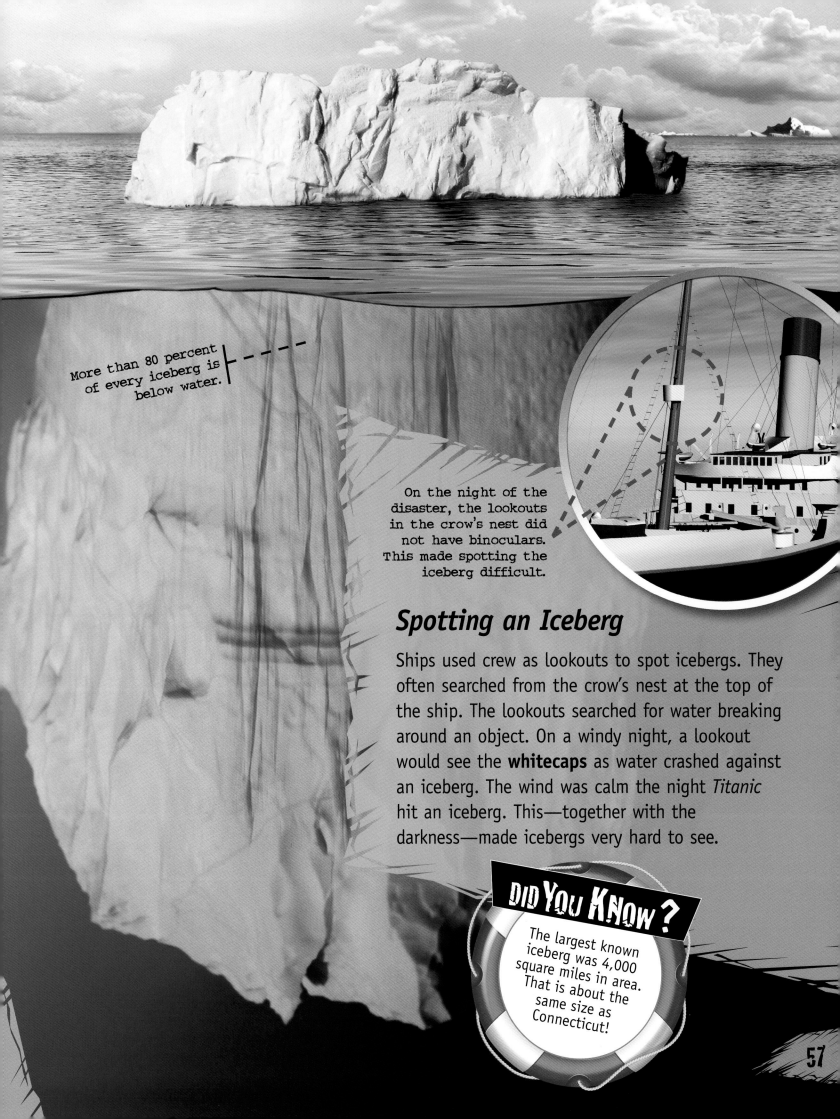

More than 80 percent of every iceberg is below water.

On the night of the disaster, the lookouts in the crow's nest did not have binoculars. This made spotting the iceberg difficult.

Spotting an Iceberg

Ships used crew as lookouts to spot icebergs. They often searched from the crow's nest at the top of the ship. The lookouts searched for water breaking around an object. On a windy night, a lookout would see the **whitecaps** as water crashed against an iceberg. The wind was calm the night *Titanic* hit an iceberg. This—together with the darkness—made icebergs very hard to see.

DID YOU KNOW?

The largest known iceberg was 4,000 square miles in area. That is about the same size as Connecticut!

DANGEROUS WATERS

Throughout the day on April 14, *Titanic's* wireless operators received numerous reports of floating ice from other ships. The reports were passed to the ship's officers, who then posted them on the bridge for all to see. But as the warnings continued to come, some did not get through to the officers, which put lives in danger.

Warning

SS Californian, a steamship owned by the Leyland Line, was in the same area as *Titanic* on the night of the disaster. It messaged *Titanic*, warning of large icebergs in the vicinity. Captain Smith was not notified because he was the guest of honor at a dinner on board. After dinner, the Captain went to the bridge and then to his cabin to sleep.

Captain Smith was an experienced sailor who had captained many liners.

Iceberg Ahead

Following warnings from other ships, two watchmen were sent up to the ship's crow's nest to look for ice, but tragically, no one was stationed at the front of the ship, where they could have spotted an iceberg sooner. Frederick Fleet, one of the watchmen, became concerned when haze made the horizon hard to see. Neither of the watchmen had binoculars. Suddenly, Fleet spotted a huge mass of ice ahead and rang the warning bell three times.

The moonless night made spotting ice difficult.

Despite ice warnings, officers kept the ship running at top speed.

DID YOU KNOW?

Passengers recalled that the air temperature fell before the collision. Some said they could smell the ice.

COLLISION

On hearing the alarm, First Officer William Murdoch stopped the ship's engines and quickly turned hard to **port** (left). This kept *Titanic* from hitting the iceberg head-on. Instead, it hit the iceberg on her **starboard** (right) side, the hull scraping along the ice.

People on deck watched helplessly as the huge iceberg loomed up toward the ship.

DID YOU KNOW?

Ice scraped from the iceberg fell on to the ship's decks. Some people picked it up and played with it.

Inspecting the Ship

Captain Smith and the ship's designer, Thomas Andrews, went below decks to inspect the damage. They moved quietly so they would not worry passengers. They discovered that the iceberg had scraped along the ship for about 300 feet. Five of Titanic's 16 watertight compartments were damaged and icy water was coming in fast. Andrews guessed they had less than two hours before the ship would sink. The wireless operators were told to contact other ships for help.

A film still showing flooding in the boiler room.

Damage

The pumps on board Titanic could get rid of 2,000 tons of water per hour, but that quantity was entering the ship every five minutes. Within ten minutes of the collision, the front five compartments of the ship were flooded to a depth of 14 feet. Within 15 minutes of the collision, the ship's post office had flooded completely.

A film still shows seawater enveloping the grand staircase.

CALLING FOR HELP

After the collision, some passengers reported smelling dampness, like in a cave. They didn't know that what they could smell was water flooding the lower part of the ship. Some were told to start loading lifeboats; many people ignored the advice because they thought the problem was temporary; others realized the ship was in trouble and put on life-jackets.

People clamored for a space on a lifeboat, as shown in this film still.

Rockets Fired

At 12:45 a.m., the crew began firing distress rockets. They should have been fired regularly every minute, but rockets from *Titanic* were fired with a gap of several minutes between each one, and from different parts of the ship. A nearby ship, *Californian*, recalled seeing flashes of light in the sky, but did not interpret these as a sign of distress and so didn't come to *Titanic*'s aid.

Titanic fired distress flares, as shown in this film still.

Wireless operator Jack Phillips sent distress signals.

Wireless Calls for Help

Titanic's Captain Smith told his wireless operator Jack Phillips to get ready to call for help while he checked the damage. It was fifteen minutes before the captain returned and ordered the calls to be made. They radioed other ships in the area, but reached only *Carpathia*. *Californian* was closer, but tragically its wireless operator was asleep in bed. After the disaster, it was recommended that all ships have wireless systems manned around the clock.

DID YOU KNOW?

Rockets have been used to send messages since the 13th century, when they were first used by Chinese armies.

63

THE FINAL MOMENTS

Chaos spread across *Titanic* as the lifeboats were lowered and the passengers began to realize that the ship was going to sink. There had never even been a lifeboat drill. Some people frantically tried to board the final lifeboat, which left around 2:05 a.m. on April 15. Survivor testimony and underwater studies tell us what we know about *Titanic's* final moments.

DID YOU KNOW?

Until the 1980s, most people thought that *Titanic* had sunk in one piece. In fact, the ship split in two before sinking.

Submerged

At about 2:10 a.m., the bow, or front, of the ship submerged, causing water to wash over the deck. Once underwater, it began to sink quickly. This caused the stern, or back, of the ship to lift into the air. Loud cracking and rumbling sounds were heard. The funnel closest to the bow collapsed at its base, crashing into the water. Soon after, the lights went out. It was about 2:17 a.m.

Breaking in Half

When the bow was fully submerged, *Titanic's* hull was under huge stress and eventually broke apart. The bow moved through the water like a torpedo. The stern turned almost on its side and slipped under the ocean. By 2:20 a.m., the whole ship was gone.

The hull split around the area of the boiler room.

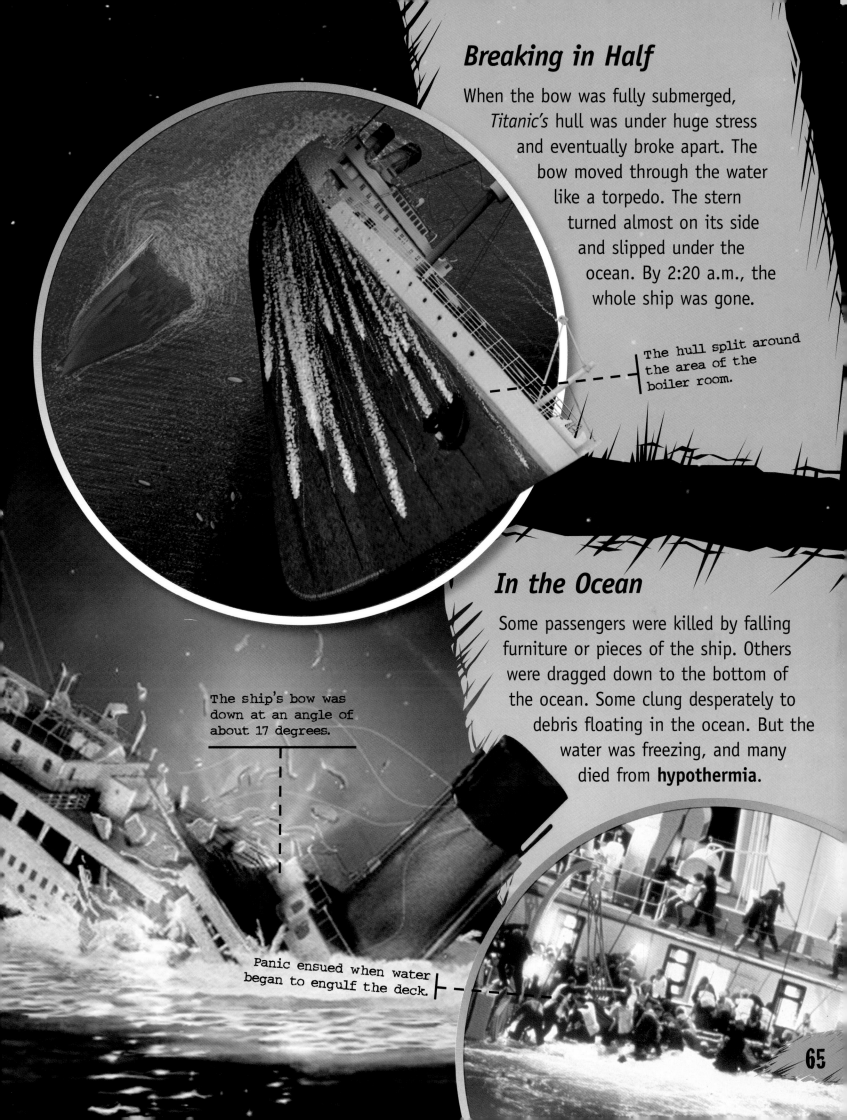

In the Ocean

Some passengers were killed by falling furniture or pieces of the ship. Others were dragged down to the bottom of the ocean. Some clung desperately to debris floating in the ocean. But the water was freezing, and many died from **hypothermia**.

The ship's bow was down at an angle of about 17 degrees.

Panic ensued when water began to engulf the deck.

LIFEBOATS

Safety regulations were very different in 1912 than they are today. There were not enough lifeboats for everyone. Still, safety inspectors said *Titanic* was safe enough for travel.

Launching each of *Titanic's* lifeboats took 10 minutes

DID YOU KNOW?

One passenger brought his dog with him when he saw there was plenty of room in the lifeboat.

Not Enough Boats

People were so convinced that *Titanic* could not sink that nobody questioned the lack of lifeboats on board. Originally, 64 lifeboats were going to be on board. This was first reduced to 32. In the end only 16 wooden lifeboats and four collapsible boats were placed aboard. This was enough for 1,178 people. There were about 2,200 passengers and crew on board.

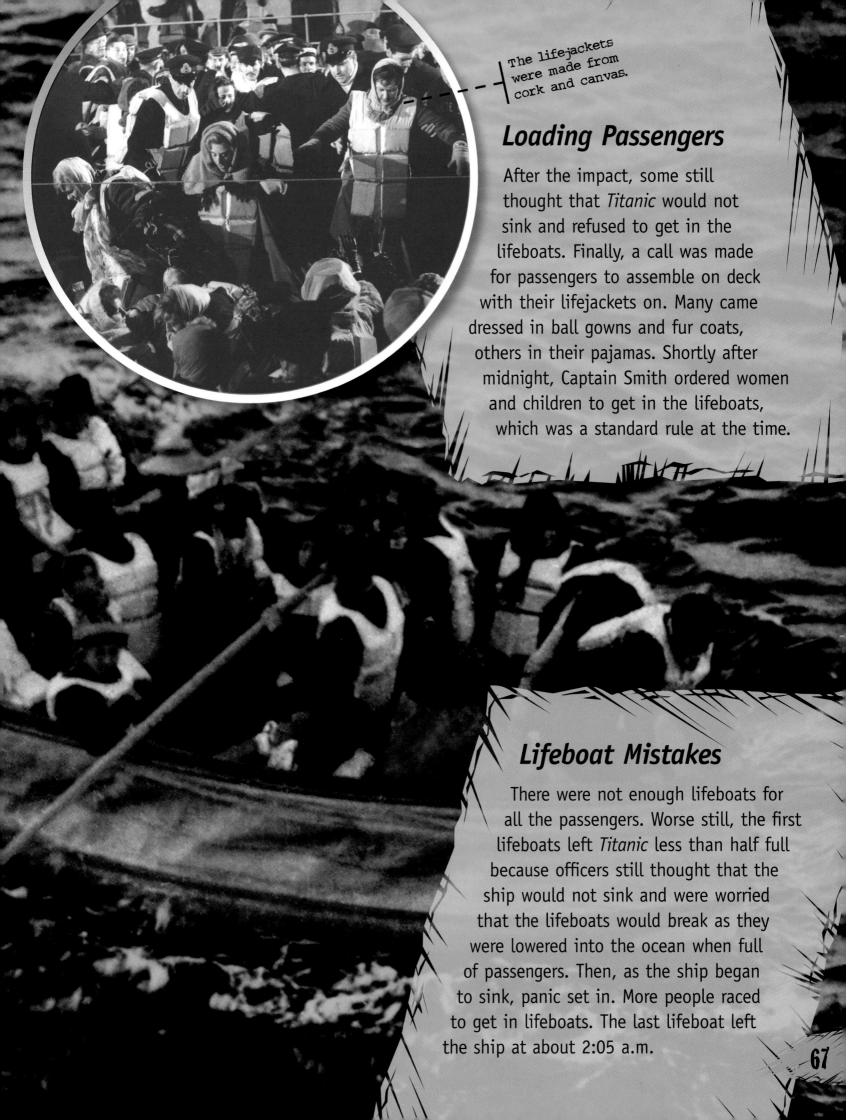

The lifejackets were made from cork and canvas.

Loading Passengers

After the impact, some still thought that *Titanic* would not sink and refused to get in the lifeboats. Finally, a call was made for passengers to assemble on deck with their lifejackets on. Many came dressed in ball gowns and fur coats, others in their pajamas. Shortly after midnight, Captain Smith ordered women and children to get in the lifeboats, which was a standard rule at the time.

Lifeboat Mistakes

There were not enough lifeboats for all the passengers. Worse still, the first lifeboats left *Titanic* less than half full because officers still thought that the ship would not sink and were worried that the lifeboats would break as they were lowered into the ocean when full of passengers. Then, as the ship began to sink, panic set in. More people raced to get in lifeboats. The last lifeboat left the ship at about 2:05 a.m.

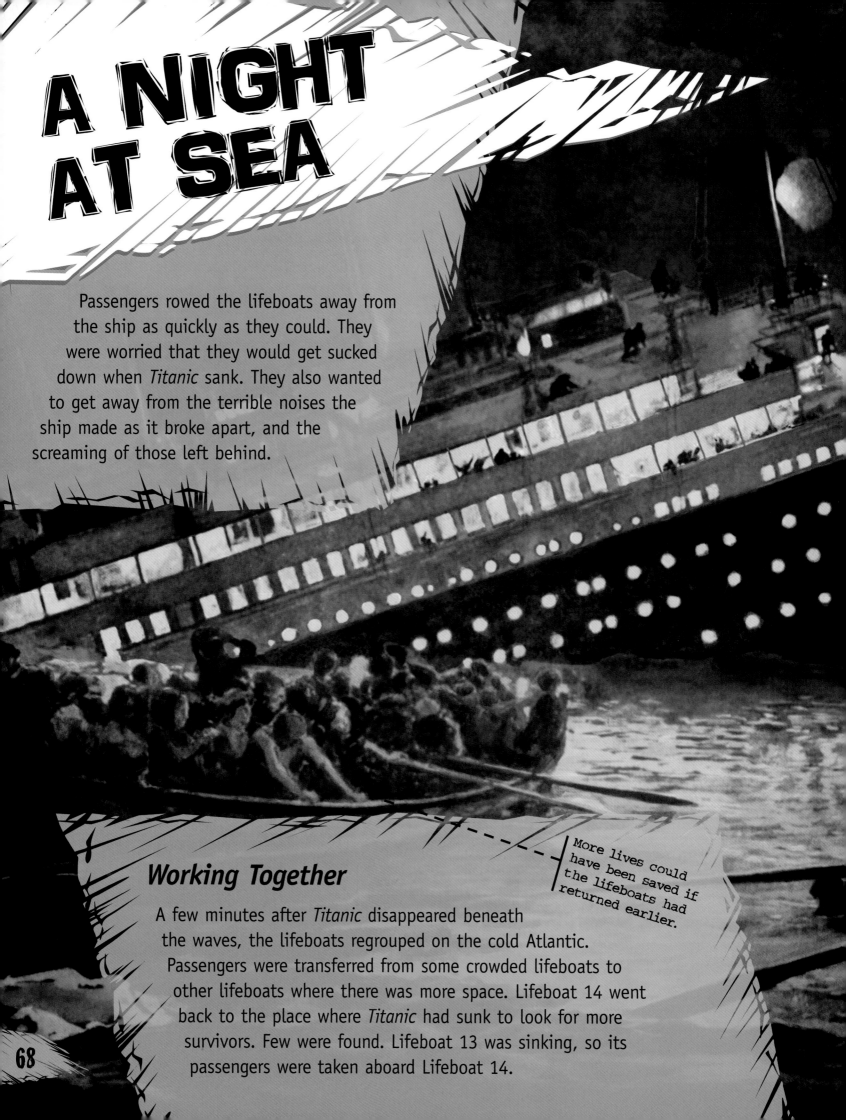

A NIGHT AT SEA

Passengers rowed the lifeboats away from the ship as quickly as they could. They were worried that they would get sucked down when *Titanic* sank. They also wanted to get away from the terrible noises the ship made as it broke apart, and the screaming of those left behind.

Working Together

A few minutes after *Titanic* disappeared beneath the waves, the lifeboats regrouped on the cold Atlantic. Passengers were transferred from some crowded lifeboats to other lifeboats where there was more space. Lifeboat 14 went back to the place where *Titanic* had sunk to look for more survivors. Few were found. Lifeboat 13 was sinking, so its passengers were taken aboard Lifeboat 14.

More lives could have been saved if the lifeboats had returned earlier.

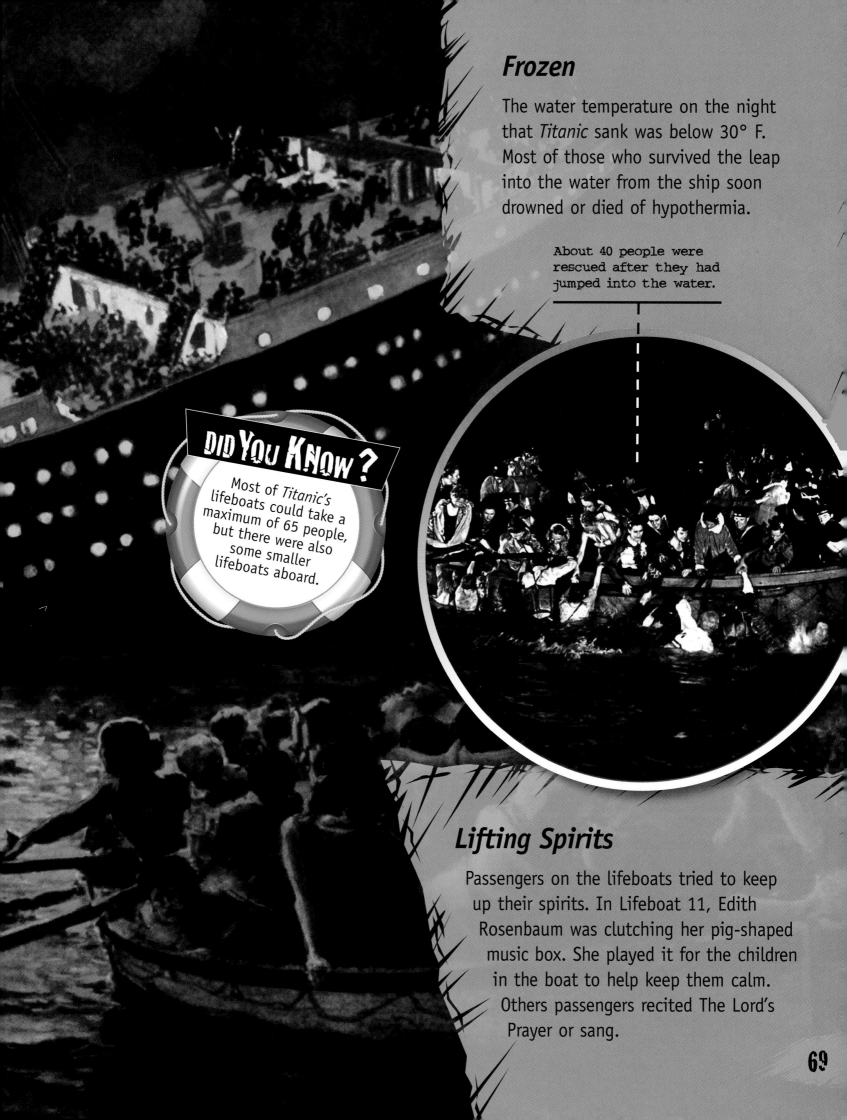

Frozen

The water temperature on the night that *Titanic* sank was below 30° F. Most of those who survived the leap into the water from the ship soon drowned or died of hypothermia.

About 40 people were rescued after they had jumped into the water.

DID YOU KNOW?

Most of *Titanic's* lifeboats could take a maximum of 65 people, but there were also some smaller lifeboats aboard.

Lifting Spirits

Passengers on the lifeboats tried to keep up their spirits. In Lifeboat 11, Edith Rosenbaum was clutching her pig-shaped music box. She played it for the children in the boat to help keep them calm. Others passengers recited The Lord's Prayer or sang.

EARLY MORNING RESCUE

The survivors spent a long night in their lifeboats, unsure if they would be rescued. They didn't know if nearby ships had received *Titanic's* distress signals. To their great relief, the *Carpathia* arrived soon. The rescue ship fired rockets to assure survivors that help was on the way.

Survivors recovered on the deck of *Carpathia*.

Carpathia was an old ship owned by the Cunard line.

Survivors Spotted

Carpathia arrived at *Titanic's* last known position at 3:30 a.m. It was dark. At first, the crew could not see the lifeboats. Then, they spotted a dim light aboard one of the lifeboats. The others soon rowed alongside. By 8:30 a.m. all the survivors were on board *Carpathia*.

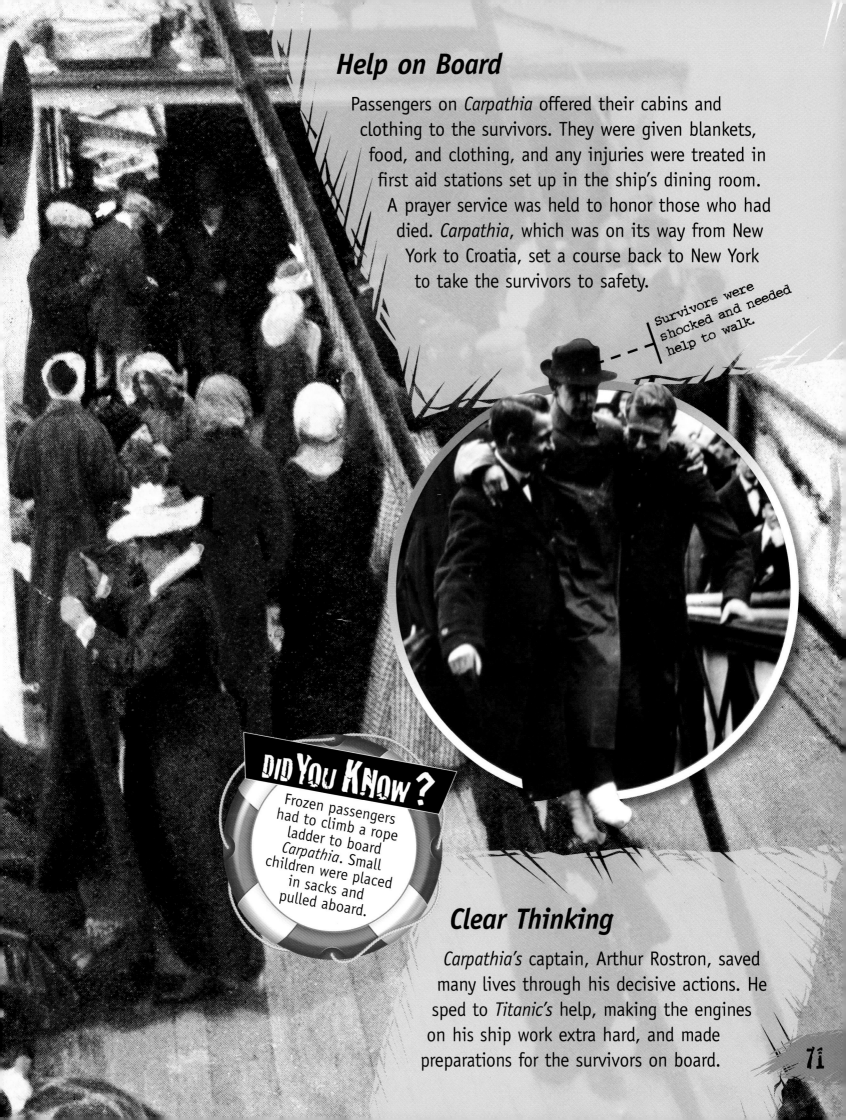

Help on Board

Passengers on *Carpathia* offered their cabins and clothing to the survivors. They were given blankets, food, and clothing, and any injuries were treated in first aid stations set up in the ship's dining room. A prayer service was held to honor those who had died. *Carpathia*, which was on its way from New York to Croatia, set a course back to New York to take the survivors to safety.

Survivors were shocked and needed help to walk.

DID YOU KNOW?

Frozen passengers had to climb a rope ladder to board *Carpathia*. Small children were placed in sacks and pulled aboard.

Clear Thinking

Carpathia's captain, Arthur Rostron, saved many lives through his decisive actions. He sped to *Titanic's* help, making the engines on his ship work extra hard, and made preparations for the survivors on board.

71

HEROES

It must have been hard to stay calm as the ship began to tilt and the passengers started to scream. But many people acted very bravely that night. Engineers, electricians, plumbers, and wireless operators worked tirelessly to save the lives of others.

The engineers could not escape and died doing their duty.

Unseen Men Down Below

Engineers stayed at their posts below decks, desperately trying to pump water out of the ship. Their goal was to keep the ship afloat until help could arrive. They prevented explosions in the boilers, and kept the lights on for as long as possible so people could find their way to the lifeboats. All 25 of them died in the tragedy.

Wireless Operators

Harold Bride and Jack Phillips (right) were in charge of the messages coming and going from *Titanic*. Upon Captain Smith's orders, they began calling nearby ships for help. They continued calling until the final moments, when nothing more could be done. Bride survived the sinking, Phillips did not.

DID YOU KNOW ?

Phillips began tapping out the letters CQD-MGY. CQD stood for "attention all stations, distress," and MGY was *Titanic's* call sign.

Passengers Help Each Other

On board, passengers helped children who could not find their parents. Some children were put on the lifeboats without their parents and were reunited with their mothers aboard *Carpathia*. Others were taken care of by other survivors until family members could come for them.

Some wives refused to leave their husbands behind.

73

LOOKING FOR LOVED ONES

In the chaos of boarding the lifeboats, families and friends became separated. When floating in the lifeboats in the darkness, survivors called out the names of their loved ones hoping to hear a response.

Survivors on *Carpathia* comforted one another.

DID YOU KNOW?

Titanic's dead are remembered to this day. Every year, a wreath is placed at the location where the magnificent ship went down.

Reunited

On board the rescue ship *Carpathia*, survivors sought out their loved ones. There were some joyful scenes when people were reunited, but many failed to find their relatives. The names of all the 705 survivors on *Carpathia* were taken so that a list could be published in newspapers once back in New York City.

A Grim Task

A cable-laying ship named *Mackay-Bennett* was sent to the site of the disaster to recover floating bodies and debris. Its crew was paid double wages to undertake this grim mission. Some of the bodies were brought back to Halifax, Nova Scotia, for burial, but some were unidentifiable and so were buried at sea.

The *Mackay-Bennett* recovered more than 300 bodies.

A monument to the dead on the Potomac in Washington.

Memorials

Churches in England and the United States held services for those who had died. Ships traveling on the same route as *Titanic* searched for objects that could be returned. In the following years, memorials to the dead were built in several cities, including Belfast, Liverpool, and Southampton in the UK, and New York and Washington D.C., U.S.

WHAT HAPPENED TO THE CREW?

Titanic's crew was 900 strong. 687 of them died in the disaster. Survivors reported that many of the crew stayed below decks to pump water out of the ship and helped passengers to find the exits. The fate of some of the surviving crew—and of others associated with the sinking—was recorded.

Frederick Fleet with other surviving crew.

Harold Bride

Bride was one of the wireless operators on Titanic. After the disaster, he continued this work on other ships during World War I. He refused to talk about events on Titanic. Eventually, he moved to Scotland where he found work as a salesman.

Frederick Fleet

Frederick Fleet was the first person to spot the iceberg. He continued working with the White Star Line and sailing on ships for 24 years. He then became a shipbuilder.

Arthur Rostron

The captain of *Carpathia*, the ship which rescued many of the survivors of the *Titanic* disaster, was given many honors. He went on to command other ships.

Rostron received the thanks of the U.S. Congress for his actions.

Stanley Lord

Stanley Lord was the captain of *Californian*, the ship that was closest to *Titanic* when it sank, but did not come to its rescue. He was forced to quit his job as a captain because some people believed he could have saved more lives. Most researchers today believe he did nothing wrong. Even if he knew of *Titanic's* peril, he probably wouldn't have been able to save many, if any, lives.

The reputation of Stanley Lord was ruined following the *Titanic* disaster.

ARRIVING IN NEW YORK

Carpathia arrived at the Cunard dock in New York.

On April 18th, three days after the *Titanic* disaster, the rescue ship *Carpathia* arrived in New York. She was greeted by small boats carrying family members and the press. More than 40,000 people had gathered on the docks to see the survivors disembark.

CARPATHIA

First days

The majority of the survivors were women and children. Most could not be comforted because their husbands and fathers were lost at sea. Many hoped another ship had come to their rescue, and they would be reunited later.

Many survivors were women and children who had boarded lifeboats.

Leaving Carpathia

Doctors and nurses waited at the docks to help passengers off the boat. Some were taken to a hospital for treatment. However, most passengers were able to walk onto the pier unassisted. It was a cold, rainy evening. Passengers were directed to tables where their details were recorded. Photographers were taking pictures, which upset many of the survivors.

There were many sad scenes on the docks when survivors disembarked.

Navigating New York

Most of the passengers had never intended to stay in New York but were on their way to other parts of the United States. Not surprisingly, many of them wished to return to their homes in America or Europe as soon as possible. In the meantime they were penniless and had nowhere to stay in a strange city. A Red Cross Emergency Relief Committee was organized to help families in need—especially those who had lost their **breadwinner**.

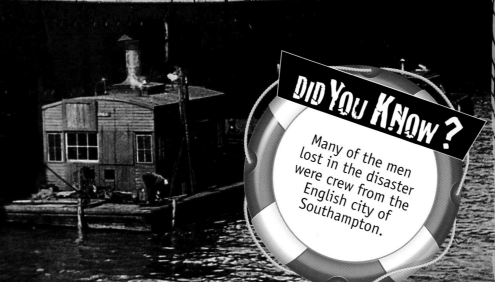

DID YOU KNOW?

Many of the men lost in the disaster were crew from the English city of Southampton.

79

MEDIA COVERAGE

The sinking of *Titanic* became a legendary story of man taking on nature—and losing. Hundreds of reporters set out to investigate the story even while *Carpathia* was on her way back to New York. At first, newspapers reported the wrong information because they didn't have survivors to interview.

Newspapers reported the sinking the day after the disaster.

Wrong Headlines

J. Bruce Ismay, the director of the White Star Line who survived the *Titanic* disaster, sent a message to his company that the ship had sunk. However, the company did not pass this information to the press right away. Confusion reigned, and some newspapers wrote that the ship was being towed for repairs and that all passengers survived.

TITANIC DISASTER GREAT LOSS OF LIFE

EVENING NEWS

LATEST NEWS~WHITE STAR "TITANIC."

Justice Davidson of Montreal Received Private Messaţ" Al
Montreal People Safe.~Among Prominent Persons Rescued
are Mrs. J. J. Astor, Countess of Rothes, Cosmo Duff Gordon

Conflicting Reports

Many of the news stories focused on the wealthiest passengers. It was hard to know which stories were true and which were false because the accident was so chaotic. Even today, there are conflicting stories of the tragic event.

Disaster Coverage

Titanic continued to be a ship of firsts, even after it lay on the ocean floor. Its sinking was the first disaster of its kind to spark such intense media interest. New technologies such as the **telegraph** and photography meant that every aspect of the story was investigated and presented to the public. The *New York Times* paid for an entire floor of a hotel to house the reporters working on the story.

The sinking of *Titanic* was front page news around the world.

SHARING STORIES

Many survivors of the disaster simply wanted to quietly resume their lives, but others wanted to tell their stories. The public had a huge appetite for these tales. Some of the stories told were true, but other passengers exaggerated the facts. Today, none of the survivors of the disaster are still alive, so all we have are records.

The survivors had fascinating tales to tell.

The disaster is the subject of countless books.

Books

One of the first books about the disaster came from survivor Archibald Gracie, who was a writer and historian. He was thought to be the last person to leave *Titanic*. He died before his book *The Truth About the Titanic* was published. Another book, *The Loss of the SS Titanic*, written by English schoolteacher Lawrence Beesley, appeared just nine weeks after the disaster.

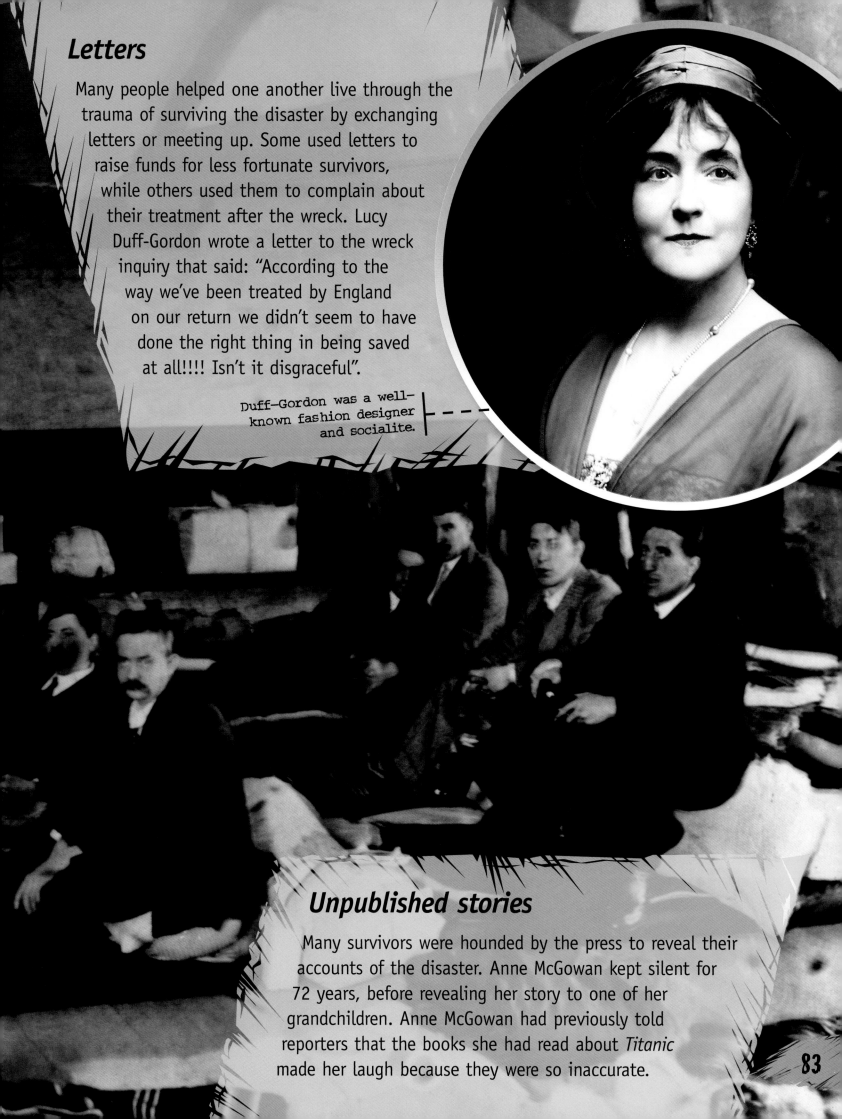

Letters

Many people helped one another live through the trauma of surviving the disaster by exchanging letters or meeting up. Some used letters to raise funds for less fortunate survivors, while others used them to complain about their treatment after the wreck. Lucy Duff-Gordon wrote a letter to the wreck inquiry that said: "According to the way we've been treated by England on our return we didn't seem to have done the right thing in being saved at all!!!! Isn't it disgraceful".

Duff-Gordon was a well-known fashion designer and socialite.

Unpublished stories

Many survivors were hounded by the press to reveal their accounts of the disaster. Anne McGowan kept silent for 72 years, before revealing her story to one of her grandchildren. Anne McGowan had previously told reporters that the books she had read about *Titanic* made her laugh because they were so inaccurate.

THE CHILDREN OF TITANIC

There were just more than 100 children on board *Titanic* when it sank. Their fate—whether or not they survived—depended on where they were on the ship. All of the children in first and second class survived the ordeal, but less than half of those in third class lived. Many children lost one or both parents in the disaster.

DID YOU KNOW?

The youngest victim of the *Titanic* disaster was Sidney Leslie Goodwin, who was just 19 months old.

Titanic Orphans

Michel and Edmond Navratil boarded *Titanic* in Southampton with their father. Their mother was in France, and did not know her sons were on the ship. When *Titanic* began to sink, they were placed in a lifeboat. Their father drowned. A survivor, Margaret Hays took care of the boys until their mother could be found.

The Youngest Survivor

Millvina Dean was just nine weeks old when she boarded *Titanic*. Her English family decided to emigrate to the U.S., seeking a new life in Kansas. When disaster struck, Millvina, her mother, and brother boarded Lifeboat 10. They survived, but her father perished. Her mother never spoke of the disaster, and Millvina didn't even know she had been on *Titanic* until she was eight years old.

Millvina Dean, the youngest survivor, lived until 2009.

Michel Navratil was only three years old when Titanic sank. His brother was two.

85

LIFE AFTER TITANIC

Many *Titanic* survivors struggled to come to terms with the trauma of the disaster and found it difficult to resume normal life. J. Bruce Ismay, the chairman of the White Star Line, for example, became a near recluse, and his wife forbade anyone to say the name "*Titanic*" in his presence.

Britannic sank with the loss of 30 lives, far fewer than *Titanic*.

Bad Luck

Violet Jessup was a stewardess on *Titanic* and survived to become a Red Cross Nurse during World War I. She served on *Titanic's* sister ship, *Britannic*, which was turned into a hospital ship during the conflict. Tragically, while sailing near the Greek island of Kea, *Britannic* struck an enemy mine and sank. Violet, though, survived the disaster by jumping into the water. She lived until the age of 83.

DID YOU KNOW?

Many *Titanic* survivors reported having repeated bad luck throughout their lives after the disaster.

Widows

Many of *Titanic's* survivors were women who lost their husbands in the disaster. Some took over their husband's businesses. Survivor Renee Harris lost her theater producer husband, Henry, in the accident. After his death, she took over New York's Hudson Theater and continued to produce successful plays. She died at the age of 93.

In Disgrace

Many people were tormented by their memories of the disaster or had their reputations ruined. Sir Cosmo Duff-Gordon and his wife escaped death in a lifeboat. However, people said that Duff-Gordon paid the crew of the lifeboat to row away from the sinking ship. People never thought the same of him again.

Duff-Gordon left in a lifeboat that was not full to capacity.

PREDICTIONS COME TRUE

The *Titanic* disaster was big news, and some people began to point out strangely accurate predictions of the ship's fate. For example, back in 1886, a highly-regarded English journalist, William Stead, had written an article titled "How the Atlantic Mail Steamer Went Down". Stead was on board *Titanic* when it sank.

DID YOU KNOW?

The Scottish politician Norman Craig decided not to sail on *Titanic*: he said "I cannot tell you why: there was simply no reason for it."

Morgan Robertson was an American writer and an experienced seaman.

A Novel

In 1898—long before *Titanic* had been imagined—author Morgan Robertson had written a short book called *Futility, or the Wrath of the Titan*. It told the story of the largest ship ever built, which sank in the Atlantic in the month of April after hitting an iceberg. There were many striking similarities between his story and the real *Titanic* disaster.

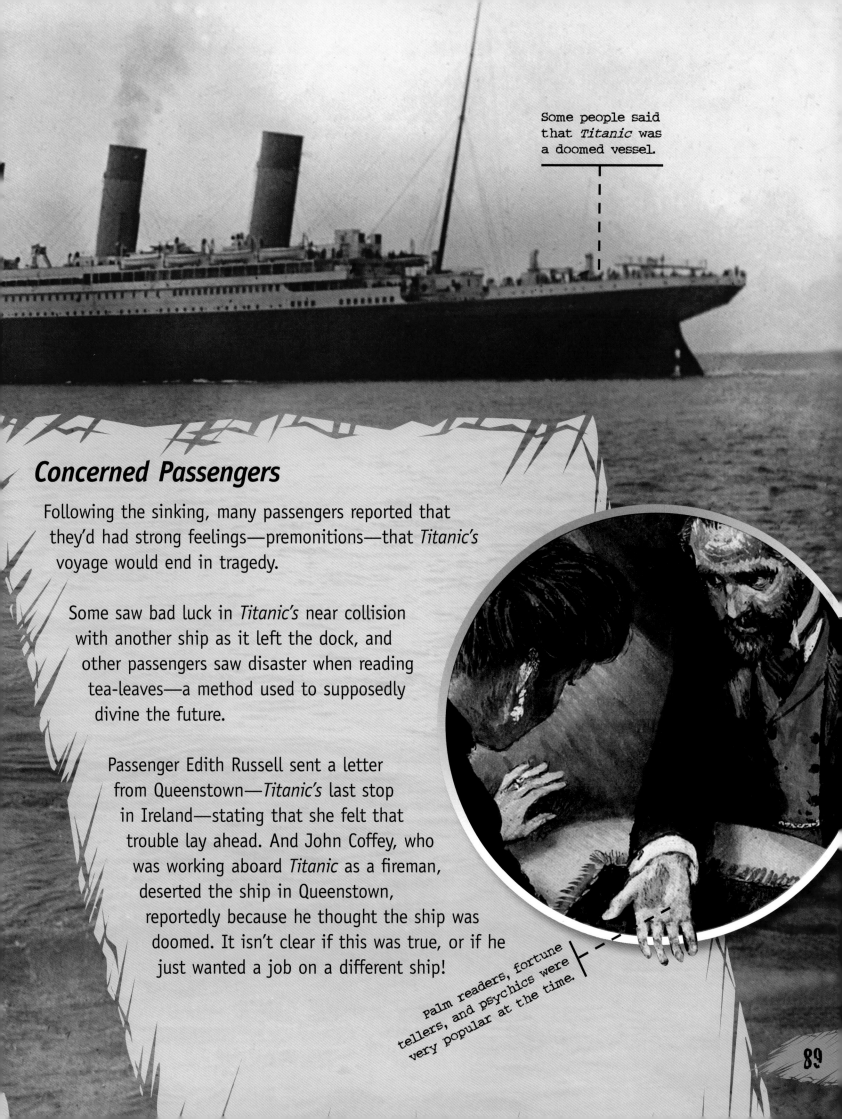

Some people said that *Titanic* was a doomed vessel.

Concerned Passengers

Following the sinking, many passengers reported that they'd had strong feelings—premonitions—that *Titanic's* voyage would end in tragedy.

Some saw bad luck in *Titanic's* near collision with another ship as it left the dock, and other passengers saw disaster when reading tea-leaves—a method used to supposedly divine the future.

Passenger Edith Russell sent a letter from Queenstown—*Titanic's* last stop in Ireland—stating that she felt that trouble lay ahead. And John Coffey, who was working aboard *Titanic* as a fireman, deserted the ship in Queenstown, reportedly because he thought the ship was doomed. It isn't clear if this was true, or if he just wanted a job on a different ship!

Palm readers, fortune tellers, and psychics were very popular at the time.

89

LUCKY CHOICES AND CLOSE CALLS

As news of *Titanic's* fate reached land, some people realized how lucky they had been. Dozens had booked passage on the ship, but for various reasons they did not board and so were spared.

Milton Hershey

The inventor of the Hershey chocolate bar spent the winter in France in 1912. He had planned to take his wife back to the U.S. in luxury on board *Titanic*. Instead left a few days earlier on the ship *Amerika*. That ship sent *Titanic* warnings of ice in the area.

Chance, fate, or a lucky decision kept some people from boarding.

Alfred Gwynne Vanderbilt

Vanderbilt was part of a very wealthy American family and traveled widely. He was booked to sail on *Titanic* but decided not to board at the last minute. Ironically, he died at sea in 1915, when the liner *Lusitania* was sunk by a German submarine.

Vanderbilt was an investor who owned valuable real estate in New York.

DID YOU KNOW?

American diplomat J.R. Mott turned down a trip on *Titanic*. He went on to receive the Nobel Peace Prize in 1946.

Guglielmo Marconi

The great Italian engineer Marconi, who had developed wireless telegraphy, was offered a ride on the maiden voyage of *Titanic*. Instead, he booked a passage for *Titanic's* second trip. His wireless device helped save the lives of more than 700 passengers. He was considered a hero.

Marconi's inventions allowed radio signals to be sent across the Atlantic.

FINAL RESTING PLACE

Titanic sank about 450 miles short of its destination of New York. It lies about 369 miles off the coast of Newfoundland in water that is 12,600 feet deep—more than eight times the height of the Empire State Building.

Where was Titanic?

When *Titanic's* wireless operators sent out distress signals as the ship was sinking, they gave the ship's position as 41.46° North and 50.14° West. Curiously, when the wreck was found decades later, this position was found to be wrong by about 13 nautical miles. It is thought that the ship's navigator made a mistake in his calculations.

Part of *Titanic* is covered by sea floor mud, as shown in this digital reconstruction.

Navigation

Today's ships use sophisticated satellite navigation to find their way across oceans, but in 1912 navigation was more difficult and less precise.

Sailors crossing the ocean used the stars as a guide, together with a technique called dead reckoning, where the ship's last position, its compass heading, and its speed were used to calculate its current position.

Titanic's compass is restored by a technician.

Debris was recovered months after the disaster.

Floating Debris

Ships passing the location of *Titanic's* grave recovered lifebelts and other objects from the ship floating on the surface of the ocean. If their owners could not be found, they were collected and stored: many items found their way into museums or private collections.

DID YOU KNOW?

Titanic's navigator, Fourth Officer Boxhall, asked for his ashes to be scattered at *Titanic's* location when he died.

THE INVESTIGATION

The American authorities wanted to know why *Titanic* had sunk and why there were not more survivors. They launched an investigation. It was run by **Senator** William Alden Smith from Michigan, who selected a panel of Senators to help with the inquiry.

The investigation looked into *Titanic*'s design.

Locating Witnesses

The Senators knew that the investigation had to start soon after the disaster, before surviving passengers and crew members set off for their homes. Important witnesses were told that they had to stay in New York for the inquiry. J. Bruce Ismay, chairman of the White Star Line, was called first to answer questions. For the next 18 days, 86 crew members and passengers were asked about the events on board.

J. Bruce Ismay and his wife leave the *Titanic* inquiry.

Witnesses reported how they were saved from death.

The Witnesses Tell All

At the investigation, witnesses were asked many questions about the speed of the boat, what they heard at the time of the crash, and how they boarded the lifeboats. The recollections of the survivors varied. Some said that boarding the lifeboats was a calm process, others said it was very chaotic. Some witnesses said that—after boarding the lifeboats—they were told that they would be back on board *Titanic* by breakfast.

British Wreck Commissioner's Inquiry

The British held their own investigation. They determined the sinking of *Titanic* was due to a collision with an iceberg, brought about by a dangerously fast speed. Careful language was used so the shipbuilders could not be sued by the victims' families.

MISTAKES

It is hard to believe that a ship that had been called "practically unsinkable" would end up at the bottom of the Atlantic Ocean just days into its maiden voyage. Formal inquiries into the disaster could not point to one single cause of the accident because many different things contributed to the disaster.

Speed and sea conditions led to the disaster.

High Speed

Titanic's Captain Smith and his officers were given many warnings of icebergs in the area. Other ships in that part of the Atlantic cut their speed because of the risk of collision. The liner *Californian* even stopped for the night. But Captain Smith continued to cruise at high speed in dangerous water. Some have speculated that the chairman of the White Star Line, who was on board, put pressure on the captain to go faster.

Short Sight

Remarkably, the lookouts in *Titanic's* crow's nest on the night of the collision did not have binoculars, and had to rely on their eyes only. This was because the binoculars were locked in a locker. The crew member who held the key to the locker had been removed from *Titanic's* crew at the last minute and had forgotten to give the key to his replacement.

Lookouts may have seen the iceberg with binoculars.

Lifeboats were said to spoil the ship's appearance.

Lifeboat Problems

When *Titanic* was built, there were no laws to make the ship's owners fit enough lifeboats for all the passengers on board. The White Star Line cut back on the number of lifeboats to give passengers more room to walk around on deck. To make matters worse, there was no lifeboat drill to tell passengers what to do in case of emergency.

DID YOU KNOW?

Watchmen were not stationed at the bow (front) of *Titanic*, where they may have spotted the iceberg earlier.

DESIGN FLAWS

Titanic was designed with watertight compartments that should have made her near-impossible to sink. The captain, Edward Smith, said: "I cannot imagine any condition which could cause [*Titanic*] to founder." Perhaps Captain Smith was too confident in the ship's design and took risks while navigating through the icebergs. Better design could have prevented the disaster.

Some said that *Titanic* should have had an additional propeller for more **maneuverability**.

A larger rudder may have helped the ship turn faster.

Steel and Power

Some people said that better materials could have saved *Titanic*. For example, using higher quality steel to make the ship's hull and rivets may have reduced the damage when it hit the iceberg. Some also said that the ship should have had more power and a bigger rudder: this may have let the officers steer clear of the iceberg once it had been sighted.

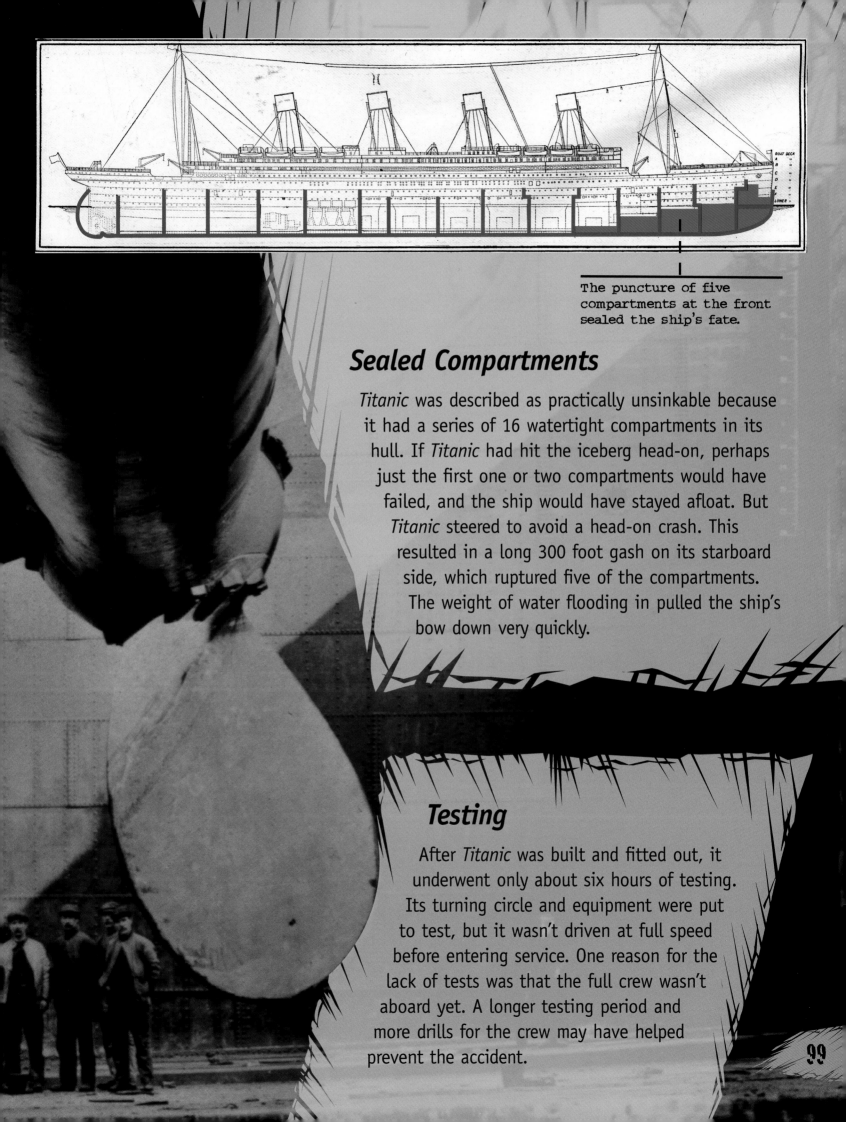

The puncture of five compartments at the front sealed the ship's fate.

Sealed Compartments

Titanic was described as practically unsinkable because it had a series of 16 watertight compartments in its hull. If *Titanic* had hit the iceberg head-on, perhaps just the first one or two compartments would have failed, and the ship would have stayed afloat. But *Titanic* steered to avoid a head-on crash. This resulted in a long 300 foot gash on its starboard side, which ruptured five of the compartments. The weight of water flooding in pulled the ship's bow down very quickly.

Testing

After *Titanic* was built and fitted out, it underwent only about six hours of testing. Its turning circle and equipment were put to test, but it wasn't driven at full speed before entering service. One reason for the lack of tests was that the full crew wasn't aboard yet. A longer testing period and more drills for the crew may have helped prevent the accident.

COULD MORE HAVE BEEN SAVED?

Californian was much smaller than Titanic.

The loss of life in the *Titanic* disaster shocked many people. They began to look for someone—or something—to blame. Attention soon focused on the actions of Captain Lord of *Californian*, the ship that was closest to *Titanic* when it sank. It had sent ice warnings to *Titanic* throughout the day.

Ignored Signals

When the sinking *Titanic* fired its distress flares, *Californian* was the nearest ship. At 12:45 a.m. on April 15, *Californian's* crew saw the flares but were not sure what they meant. *Californian's* Captain Lord did not respond. The ship's wireless operator had gone to sleep, so the crew found out about Titanic's fate the next morning. By then, *Carpathia* had already picked up all of the survivors.

The crew of Californian were questioned at the Titanic inquiry.

Distorted View

Crew on the *Californian* saw lights flashing in the distance. These were probably signaling lamps on *Titanic* sending distress messages in Morse code. Unfortunately, the signals were not recognized and the *Californian* did not know a message was being sent.

A signaling lamp recovered from *Titanic.*

Could Californian Have Helped?

Titanic was between 8 and 22 miles away from *Californian* when it began to sink. Some people think *Californian* should have gone to *Titanic's* aid. But even if the ships had been within 8 miles of each other, *Californian* would have arrived at the disaster scene at 2:45 a.m., by which time *Titanic* was already below the ocean.

DID YOU KNOW ?

Caption Lord ordered *Californian* to stop for the night because he thought it too dangerous to travel through an icefield in the dark.

TITANIC FORGOTTEN

After the *Titanic* disaster, many people wanted to find and recover the wreck. Some proposed using powerful magnets to locate and pick up the steel hull. The start of World War I in 1914 soon made people forget about *Titanic* and focus instead on world events.

Navies played a big role in both World Wars.

World War I

In June 1914, World War I dominated the news and few thought about *Titanic*. Millions of men ware drafted into armies—some countries sent 80 percent of their men to fight. The war lasted four years.

The Great Depression

After World War I, many countries faced economic hardships. In the Great Depression between 1929 and 1939, one in four people in the U.S. lost their jobs. There was little interest in the *Titanic* disaster and no money to search for the wreck.

Food aid was given to the poor in the depression.

World War II saw US soldiers fighting in Japan.

World War II

War broke out again in 1939 and lasted until 1945. Millions of men were sent to battle. News was focused on the war and tragedies that were occurring in Europe. *Titanic* was largely forgotten.

TITANIC FEVER

After the end of World War II in 1945, interest in *Titanic* was renewed by books, television, and especially movies. The disaster has been the subject of scores of movies.

A poster for the 1953 movie *Titanic* shows the disaster.

Titanic on Film

A handful of movies about *Titanic* had been made before the end of World War II, including a Nazi propaganda film that showed the British as villains and a German officer as a hero on board. The first American post-war film was *Titanic*, starring Clifton Webb and Barbara Stanwyck. The film showed the main events fairly accurately, though details of people were not all correct. It was considered well-researched for its time.

A Night to Remember

The writer Walter Lord wanted to produce a minute-by-minute account of what passengers went through on *Titanic*. He interviewed many of the ship's survivors, and learned as much as he could about the disaster. His 1955 book, *A Night to Remember*, became a best-seller soon after it was published and was made into a successful movie in 1958. It is considered to be a reasonably accurate account of events.

Captain Smith talks to his second officer in *A Night to Remember*.

DID YOU KNOW ?

Director Alfred Hitchcock wanted to make a movie about *Titanic* in 1939, but the studios advised against it.

ROBERT **WAGNER** · AUDREY **DALTON** · THELMA **RITT**

with BRIAN **AHERNE** · RICHARD **BASEHART**

NEW TECHNOLOGY

The people looking for the wreck of *Titanic* knew approximately where it lay. However, the ship had inaccurately transmitted its coordinates just before it sank. Finding *Titanic* in deep waters in the Atlantic, where the weather was often rough, would be no easy matter. It depended on new technologies, such as sonar.

DID YOU KNOW?

Sonar was developed for use by the navy during World War I. It helped sailors locate enemy submarines.

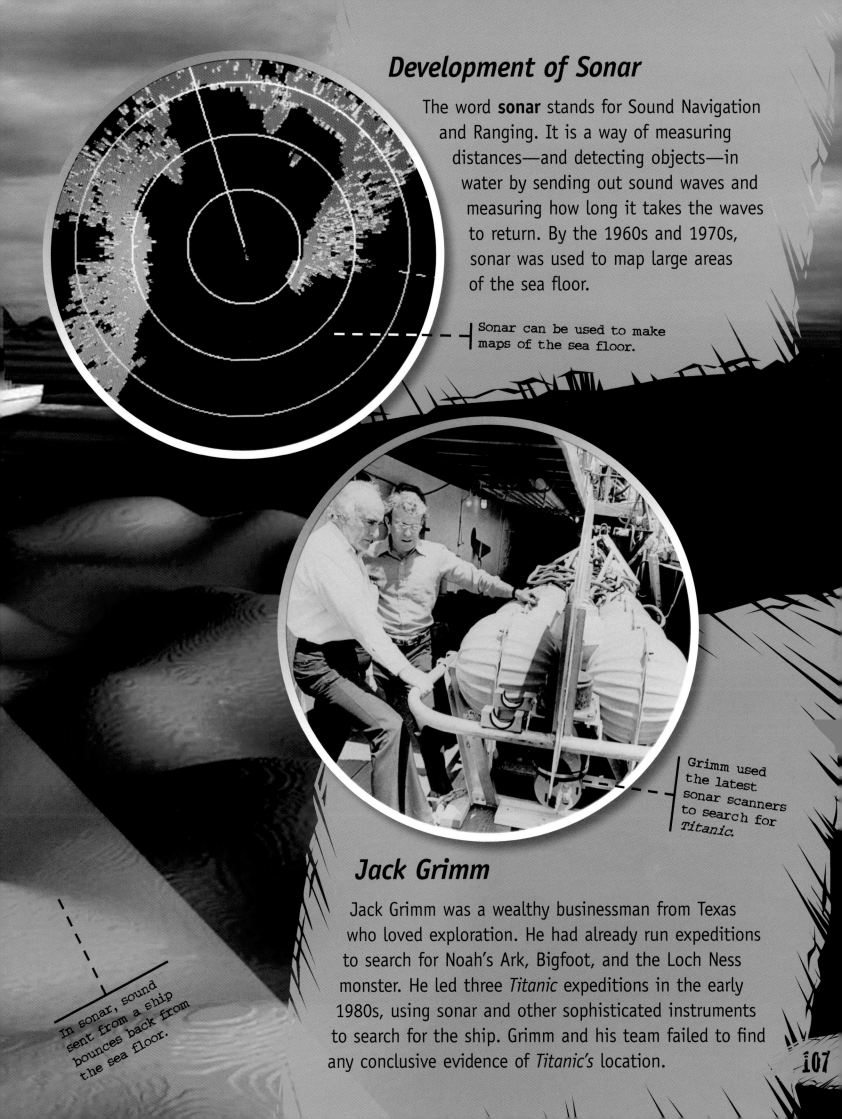

Development of Sonar

The word **sonar** stands for Sound Navigation and Ranging. It is a way of measuring distances—and detecting objects—in water by sending out sound waves and measuring how long it takes the waves to return. By the 1960s and 1970s, sonar was used to map large areas of the sea floor.

Sonar can be used to make maps of the sea floor.

Grimm used the latest sonar scanners to search for *Titanic.*

Jack Grimm

Jack Grimm was a wealthy businessman from Texas who loved exploration. He had already run expeditions to search for Noah's Ark, Bigfoot, and the Loch Ness monster. He led three *Titanic* expeditions in the early 1980s, using sonar and other sophisticated instruments to search for the ship. Grimm and his team failed to find any conclusive evidence of *Titanic's* location.

In sonar, sound sent from a ship bounces back from the sea floor.

107

GETTING CLOSER

As scientists and researchers began to investigate the ocean depths, and new techniques were developed to locate and salvage sunken ships and submarines, it became more likely that the wreck of *Titanic* would finally be found.

DID YOU KNOW?

Titanic lay in water about 12,600 feet deep. The deepest water on Earth is 36,000 feet in the Pacific Ocean.

A model of the bathyscaphe shows its cigar shape.

The Thresher Discovery

In 1963, the accidental sinking of a nuclear submarine named the *USS Thresher* inspired new techniques in seabed search and rescue. *Thresher* rested at a depth of 8,400 feet (about two-thirds as deep as *Titanic*). The U.S. Navy lowered a bathyscaphe—a deep-water vessel —to look for *Thresher*. The bathyscaphe located *Thresher* and took photos.

Unmanned Submarines

Deep-sea archaeologist and oceanographer Robert D. Ballard had been involved in the search for *Thresher*. An expert on shipwrecks, he developed an advanced search submarine or **remotely operated vehicle** (ROV), named *Argo*. Fitted with cameras and searchlights, this unmanned vehicle could be towed behind a ship at a depth of up to 20,000 feet.

Robert Ballard planned every mission of *Argo* very carefully.

The search vehicle *Argo* was towed by a ship.

THE HUNT FOR TITANIC

Robert Ballard studied the ways in which shipwrecks left behind trails of debris on the sea floor. He teamed up with Jean-Louis Michel, one of the leaders in undersea exploration. They started to look for the telltale traces of debris that would lead them to *Titanic*.

Closing In

First, Ballard and Michel decided on the area in which they would search. They started with the coordinates given by *Titanic* as she sank. They then took into account the direction of water currents in the Atlantic at the time, and also the position at which *Carpathia* found the survivors in the lifeboats. They searched this area on board a ship named *Knorr*, which towed the submarine *Argo* that Ballard had designed.

The research ship *Knorr* was used in the hunt for Titanic.

Found It!

73 years, 4 months, and 17 days after *Titanic* slipped below the surface, it was rediscovered. At 12:48 a.m. on September 1, 1985 Michel, Ballard, and the crew saw telltale metallic debris in their video monitors. About ten minutes later, a gigantic boiler came into view. Michel checked a photograph of *Titanic's* engine room. The boiler matched the photo. *Titanic* had been found!

The boiler's shape helped to identify the wreck.

FIRST SIGHTS

Ballard and his team of explorers looked closely at *Titanic's* exterior and took a lot of photos of the hull and of twisted metal, railings, and portholes on the ocean floor. They didn't have as much time to explore as they would have liked, because their ship, *Knorr* was needed for other missions.

This photo shows windows of the office quarters on board the ship.

Return to the Wreck

Ballard and his team came back to the wreck in 1986 with new technology that let them explore the ship in more detail. They brought a submersible named *Alvin*, and a smaller remote camera system named *Jason Junior*. This could be steered into small holes in the ship, allowing people to see *Titanic's* interior.

Jason Junior could work at depths that would have crushed other gear.

This photo shows china dishes, still neatly stacked, on the sea bed.

Remembering the Dead

During his first two expeditions to *Titanic*, Robert Ballard did not bring any objects to the surface. He thought of the wreck as a cemetery, and felt that he and others should respect the memory of those who had died there. At first, Ballard had even wanted to keep the location of the wreck a secret.

DID YOU KNOW?

Wine bottles, coal, bedsprings, windows, and plates were found scattered over a square mile around the ship.

TWO BIG PIECES

The early explorations by Ballard and Michel confirmed what many people had thought—that *Titanic* had split into two pieces before it sank. The stern, which was broken up and badly damaged, lay on the sea floor about 2,000 feet away from the bow, which was in much better condition.

BOW

The bow, or front, of the ship was rusted but otherwise intact.

The Bow

The bow of the ship was well preserved. As it sank, water filled the "watertight" chambers at the bow. The front of the ship became heavy, causing the stern to rise into the air. The steel plates of the hull failed, and the enormous ship broke in two.

The bow sank to the bottom. Water was already inside this part of the ship when it sank, so the bow held its shape. It looked much the same after decades underwater as it did in 1912.

STERN

The Stern

As *Titanic* was sinking, the stern twisted and fell under the water quickly. There was still air in the lower levels of the ship. As it went under, the pressure from the water pushed on the walls of the ship and crushed it.

The railings on the stern of the ship are still intact and visible.

RAISING TITANIC

By the 1960s, interest in *Titanic* had come back again. Most people wrongly believed that the ship was intact in one piece at the bottom of the ocean. Some made ambitious plans to locate and salvage *Titanic* and turn it into a tourist attraction.

Titanic had in fact split into two before sinking.

Refloating the Ship

Some wild ideas were suggested to raise the *Titanic*. One involved using a diving vessel to attach gas-filled nylon balloons to the hull; others proposed freezing the ship, which would then float to the surface like a giant ice cube. Some people wanted to salvage *Titanic* and turn it into a floating museum, like other museum ships.

Raising *Titanic* was the subject of a movie in 1980.

Desperate Ideas

One *Titanic* enthusiast thought the ship could be raised by filling the hull with ping-pong balls to make it float. Others believed that the hull could be brought to the surface by pumping it full of wax, which is less dense than water and floats. Others still suggested blowing up the hull and have it come up in pieces.

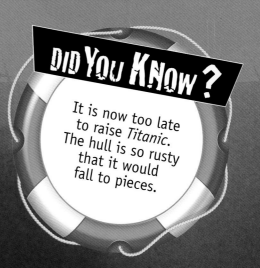

DID YOU KNOW?

It is now too late to raise *Titanic*. The hull is so rusty that it would fall to pieces.

ANSWERING QUESTIONS

In 1986, the Discovery Channel made a documentary film about *Titanic*. They assembled a group of scientists and engineers to answer questions about its sinking. Naval architects, oceanographers, recovery experts, microbial biologists, metals scientists, and historians were just a few of the experts brought along to analyze evidence.

What Made It Sink?

Everyone wanted to know what caused the sinking of the most advanced ship of the time, and how such a huge vessel could have sunk so quickly. Studies showed that the hull failed because it had components made from poor grade steel, which was made even more brittle by the very cold sea temperature.

The engine room of *Titanic* can be seen through a hole in the hull.

The heads of the rivets would have snapped off in the collision.

Brittle Rivets

One problem affected the ship's rivets—the metal pins that held the plates of its steel hull together. **Metallurgists** took samples of the rivets directly from the wreck of *Titanic* and studied them under a microscope. They noticed that the steel had imperfections that made it weak. Instead of bending under the great stress of a collision, the rivets would have shattered, like plates being hit with a hammer. This is what caused the catastrophic and rapid failure of *Titanic's* hull.

Ice cold water made the steel hull very brittle, and prone to shatter.

DID YOU KNOW?

Steel plates were once riveted together to make the hull. In modern ships, they are welded for extra strength.

LESSONS LEARNED

The *Titanic* disaster brought about major changes in the design and operation of ships. The International Convention for the Safety of Life at Sea was held soon after the tragedy, and as a result sailing is now a much safer form of travel.

DID YOU KNOW?

Lifeboats today must be capable of being loaded, launched, and steered away from the ship in 30 minutes.

Iceberg Patrol

Today's ships must have enough lifeboats for all passengers, and their radios must be monitored 24 hours a day. An organization named International Ice Patrol now patrols the Atlantic to warn of icebergs and record their sizes and positions.

A U.S. ship carries out an ice patrol in the Arctic.

Lifeboats line the decks of a modern cruise liner.

Flares

Before *Titanic* sank, countries used distress flares in different ways. After the disaster, the way flares were used as signals was standardized across all countries. Radio communication is now very advanced and strict safety standards are followed.

Construction

Titanic was a stark reminder that nothing is indestructible. Steel used in modern ships is stronger and welded together, not held in place by rivets. Scientists who study metal have found ways of building ships to withstand cold temperatures.

Welded joints make stronger hulls and safer ships.

DECAYING TITANIC

Time to recover objects from *Titanic's* watery grave is running out. Some scientists predict that the hull will continue to get eaten away by corrosion and microbes and will collapse by the year 2030. Others say it may last for another hundred years.

Rusticles

Much of the damage to iron objects on *Titanic*—including the hull—is being caused by microscopic bacteria. They feed on the iron in the steel plates of the ship, forming structures that look like rusty icicles inside and outside the wreck. These orange-red structures have been called "rusticles."

A lifeboat winch on *Titanic's* deck is being eaten away and covered in rusticles.

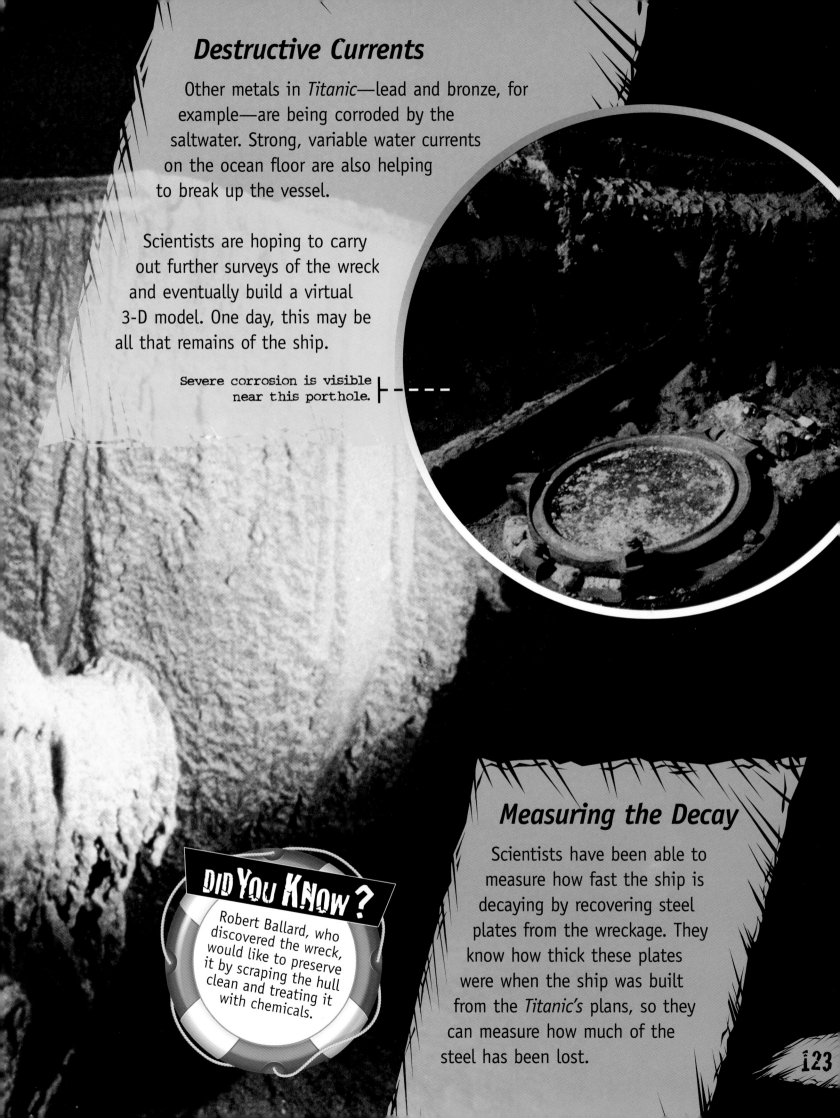

Destructive Currents

Other metals in *Titanic*—lead and bronze, for example—are being corroded by the saltwater. Strong, variable water currents on the ocean floor are also helping to break up the vessel.

Scientists are hoping to carry out further surveys of the wreck and eventually build a virtual 3-D model. One day, this may be all that remains of the ship.

Severe corrosion is visible near this porthole.

DID YOU KNOW?

Robert Ballard, who discovered the wreck, would like to preserve it by scraping the hull clean and treating it with chemicals.

Measuring the Decay

Scientists have been able to measure how fast the ship is decaying by recovering steel plates from the wreckage. They know how thick these plates were when the ship was built from the *Titanic's* plans, so they can measure how much of the steel has been lost.

123

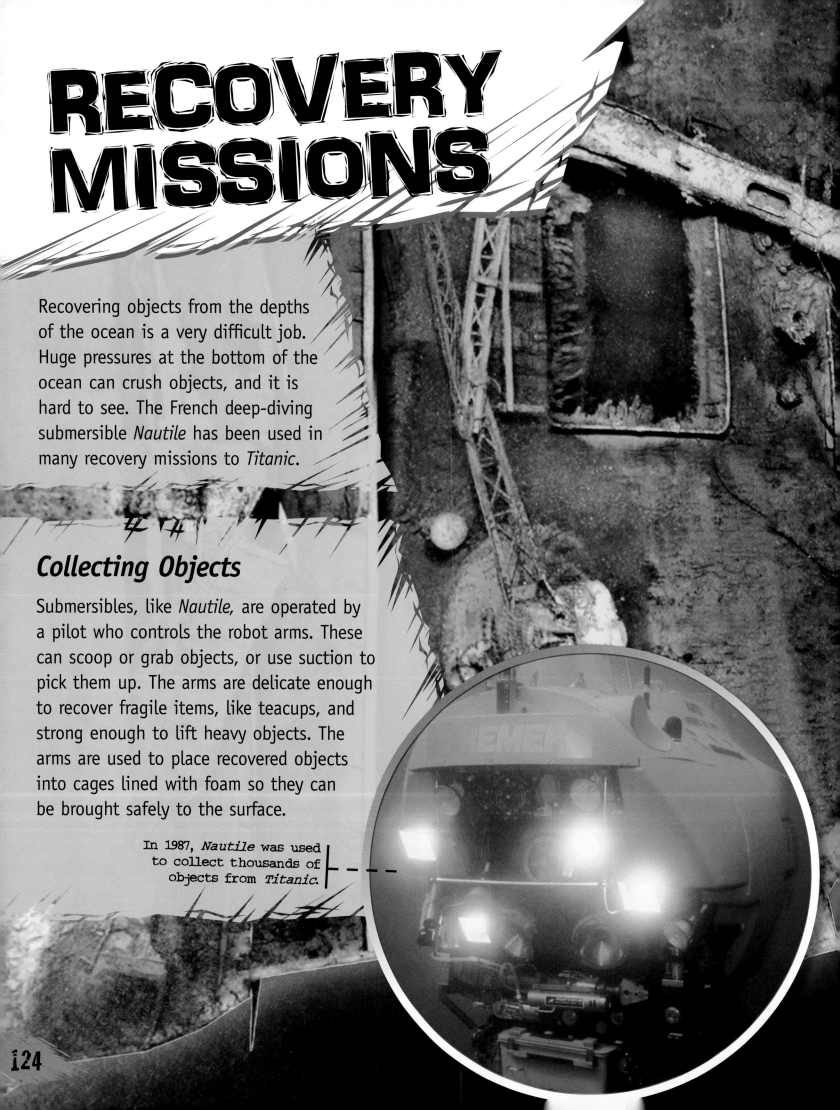

RECOVERY MISSIONS

Recovering objects from the depths of the ocean is a very difficult job. Huge pressures at the bottom of the ocean can crush objects, and it is hard to see. The French deep-diving submersible *Nautile* has been used in many recovery missions to *Titanic*.

Collecting Objects

Submersibles, like *Nautile*, are operated by a pilot who controls the robot arms. These can scoop or grab objects, or use suction to pick them up. The arms are delicate enough to recover fragile items, like teacups, and strong enough to lift heavy objects. The arms are used to place recovered objects into cages lined with foam so they can be brought safely to the surface.

In 1987, *Nautile* was used to collect thousands of objects from *Titanic*.

Mapping the Crash

Researchers have stitched together many images to build up a map of the crash site. They have discovered that *Titanic* actually lies in three pieces—the bow and stern and a third, middle section of the ship. Whenever objects are discovered and collected, their position is noted on the map.

Robert Ballard stands in front of a photograph of the upper deck.

RESTORING OBJECTS

Titanic lies deep on the ocean floor where there is hardly any oxygen, and the temperature is close to freezing. This has helped to preserve objects within the wreck. However, salt, acids, and organisms in the water are working constantly to break things down.

Objects are hauled from the wreck in cages.

DID YOU KNOW?

Objects from *Titanic* are sought after by collectors. A lunch menu recovered from the ship sold for $122,000.

Handle with Care

Sea water corrodes metal objects, especially those made of iron and copper. When metal objects are brought to the surface, they are treated with chemicals to stop them from rusting. Leather, paper, and wood objects break apart quickly, too. They are treated with a special preserving solution and carefully cleaned with a soft brush.

A restoration technician works on a leather bag from the wreck.

Priceless Memories

Some of the most precious and interesting items recovered from *Titanic* are the letters, books, and journals of its passengers. Even these delicate objects have been restored and made readable after eighty years in the ocean. To do this, the paper is freeze-dried to remove all the water. Then, it is chemically treated and placed in a room where the temperatures can be closely controlled.

A well preserved London bus ticket, recovered from the wreck.

EXHIBITS

There are many debates about who owns the objects in wrecks at the bottom of the ocean. Some believe the objects should remain undisturbed, others say that they should be shared as a part of our international culture and history.

An 18 foot model of Titanic in Missouri

Museums in the United States

Almost every state in America has a museum that includes artifacts from the *Titanic*. New York City is especially rich with *Titanic* history and has three museums which include objects from the ship. The National Museum of American History in Washington D.C. has a permanent display of *Titanic* artifacts. The *Titanic* Museum in Branson, Missouri includes a replica of the ship's grand staircase and cabins. In Denver, Colorado, a museum is dedicated to the "Unsinkable" Molly Brown.

A woman poses as Molly Brown in a museum in Denver, Colorado.

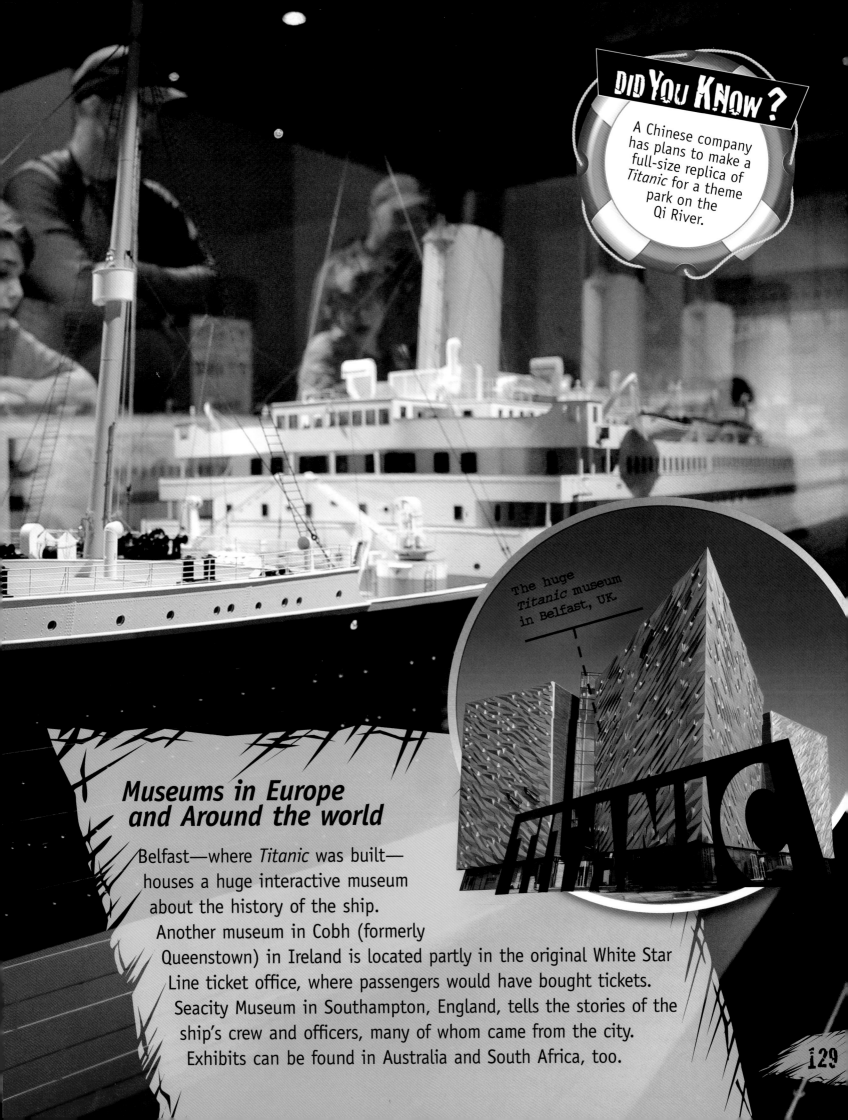

The huge *Titanic* museum in Belfast, UK.

Museums in Europe and Around the world

Belfast—where *Titanic* was built— houses a huge interactive museum about the history of the ship.

Another museum in Cobh (formerly Queenstown) in Ireland is located partly in the original White Star Line ticket office, where passengers would have bought tickets.

Seacity Museum in Southampton, England, tells the stories of the ship's crew and officers, many of whom came from the city.

Exhibits can be found in Australia and South Africa, too.

TITANIC ENTERTAINMENT

Public interest in Titanic remains as big as the ship itself. Hundreds of books have been written about the ill-fated liner. Movies continue to be made and there is even a musical about the disaster.

Movies

The most recent Titanic movie was released in 1997. It cost more than $200 million to make. Director James Cameron used the names of some of the real passengers, and took some of his facts from the Titanic Investigation, but most of the story was made up. The movie was best known for its special effects.

Cameron's film used replicas of the ship, its cabins, and staircase. It took 5 million gallons of water to recreate the flooding of the ship's staircase during filming. The movie set was built in Mexico and some of it still remains and can be viewed.

The movie starred Kate Winslet and Leonardo di Caprio.

The musical *Titanic* toured many countries, including Germany.

The Musical

After the success of James Cameron's movie in 1997, a musical was created for Broadway in New York. New technology was used to create a sinking ship on stage. Like in the real *Titanic*, the technology did not always work, but the production was considered a success.

DID YOU KNOW?

James Cameron's *Titanic* won 11 Oscar Awards, including Best Picture and Best Visual Effects.

TITANIC MEMORABILIA

People are still fascinated by events surrounding the *Titanic* disaster. Collectors have paid large sums of money for items recovered from the shipwreck, or associated with the ship, such as deck plans and photographs.

Auctions

Personal letters and correspondence on White Star Line notepaper have sold for more than $150,000. Auctions of *Titanic* memorabilia always attract a lot of media interest, but never more so than in 2012—the **centenary** of the *Titanic* disaster.

Photo of the Iceberg

One of the most amazing photographs connected with the disaster was taken by W.F. Wood—the captain of the *SS Estonian*—two days after *Titanic's* sinking. It is believed to be a picture of the iceberg that hit *Titanic* because the iceberg had red paint smeared along its bottom.

Rare photos, such as this picture of the iceberg that *Titanic* hit, are in great demand.

An auction of memorabilia in New York.

Hartley's Violin

The violin that belonged to Wallace Hartley, *Titanic's* bandleader, was played on deck as the ship sank. It was believed to have survived in a bag strapped onto Hartley's body. Then it was recovered by his fiancée. It took experts seven years to prove beyond a doubt that the violin was genuine. It sold at auction for a staggering $1,300,000 in 2013.

Hartley's violin remained in good condition.

133

OTHER SHIPWRECKS

Titanic is perhaps the most famous shipwreck in history, but it is just one of many ships lost at sea. Some wrecks are thousands of years old, and all tell stories of exploration, war, and adventure. Many are deteriorating at the bottom of the ocean, though there are efforts to preserve the most important.

DID YOU KNOW?

More than 29 million people have been to see *Vasa*. That makes it the most viewed shipwreck in history.

Arizona exploded when hit by Japanese bombs.

USS Arizona

This U.S. battleship sailed from California to Pearl Harbor, Hawaii, to deter a predicted Japanese attack. The ship was bombed by Japanese planes and sank. Most of the wreck remains in the harbor to this day.

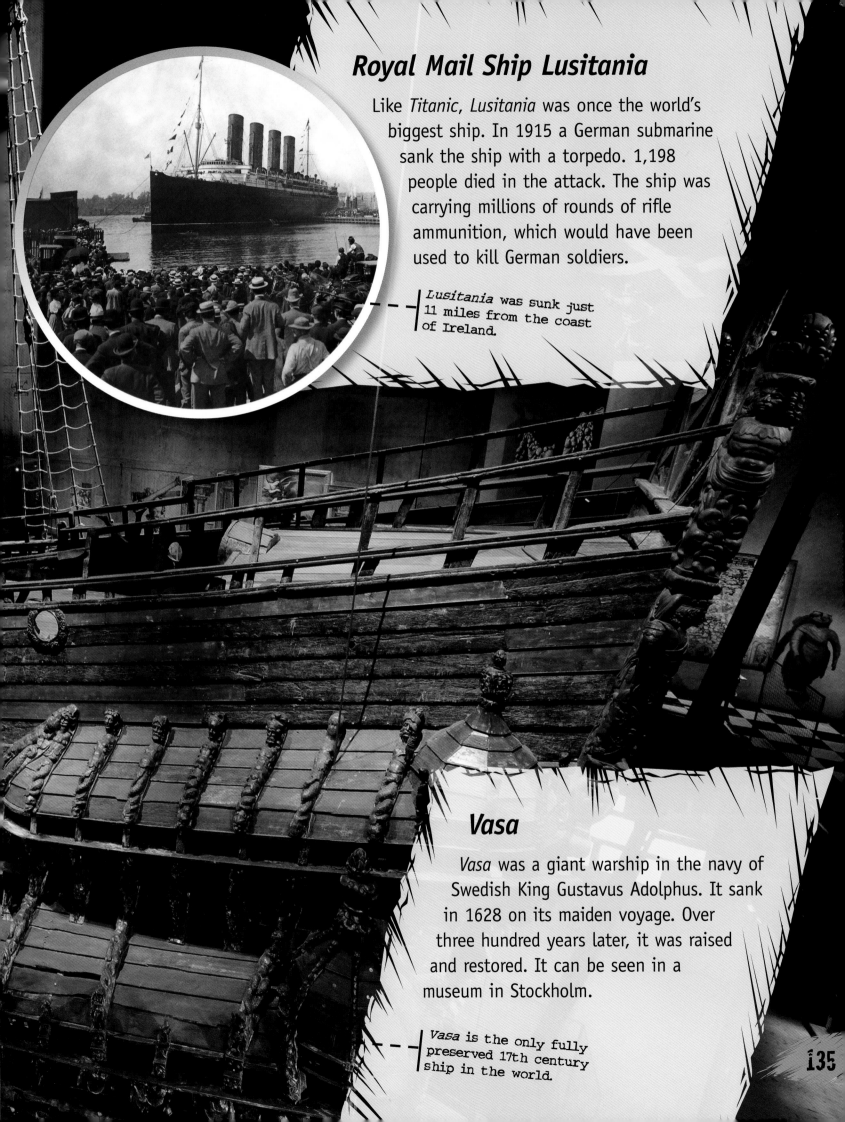

Royal Mail Ship Lusitania

Like *Titanic*, *Lusitania* was once the world's biggest ship. In 1915 a German submarine sank the ship with a torpedo. 1,198 people died in the attack. The ship was carrying millions of rounds of rifle ammunition, which would have been used to kill German soldiers.

Lusitania was sunk just 11 miles from the coast of Ireland.

Vasa

Vasa was a giant warship in the navy of Swedish King Gustavus Adolphus. It sank in 1628 on its maiden voyage. Over three hundred years later, it was raised and restored. It can be seen in a museum in Stockholm.

Vasa is the only fully preserved 17th century ship in the world.

CRUISE SHIPS TODAY

With international air travel now relatively inexpensive, very few people choose to cross the Atlantic or travel long distances by ship. However, cruising—sightseeing from a luxury ship—is a big industry. Giant cruise lines carry people on tours as far away as the Antarctic.

Luxury Liners

Today's cruise ships are even more luxurious than Titanic. They have swimming pools, climbing walls, and other fantastic sports facilities. Restaurants, casinos, and live shows provide entertainment.

MAJESTY of the SEAS

Facilities on cruise ships are often better than on land

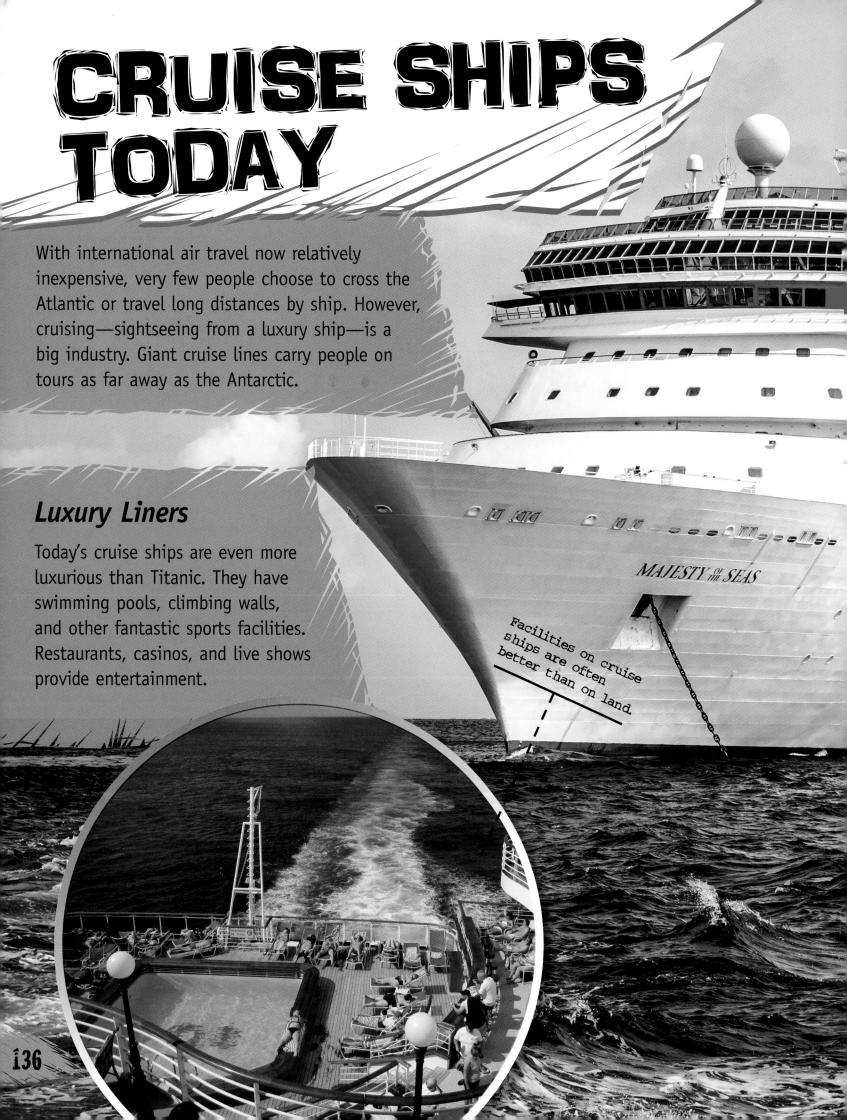

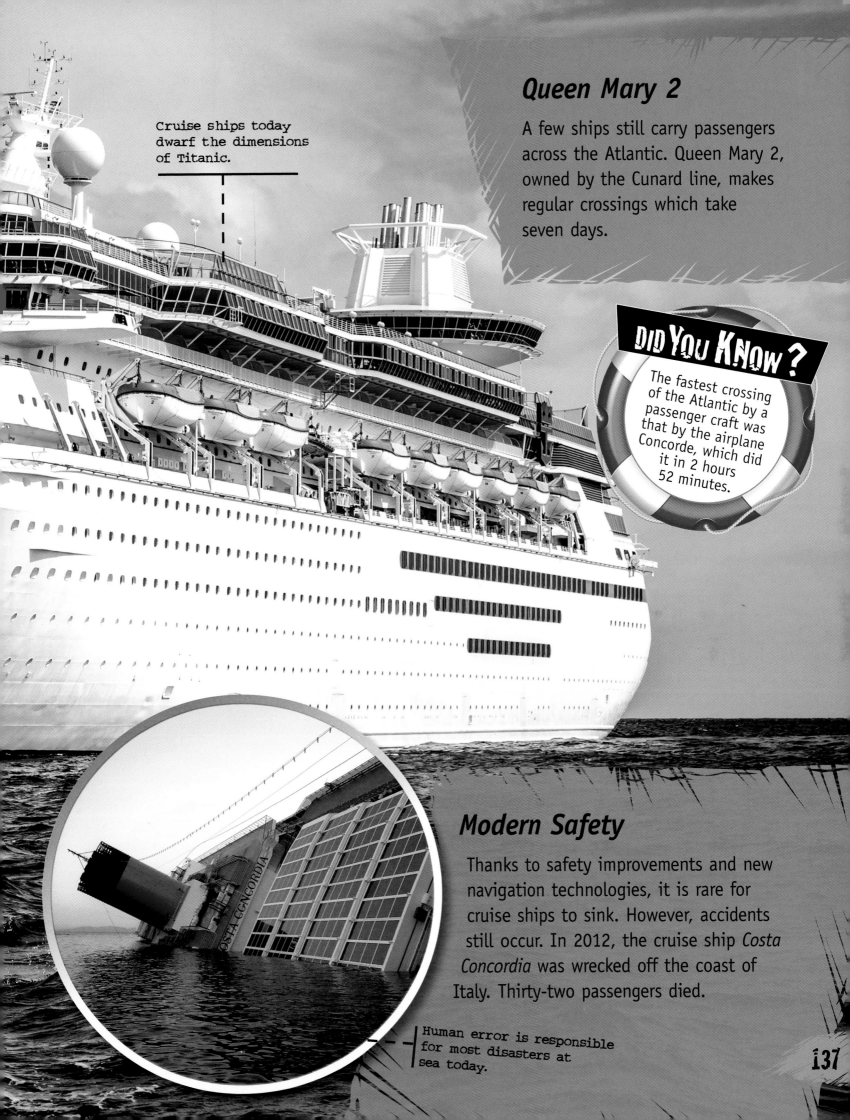

Cruise ships today dwarf the dimensions of Titanic.

Queen Mary 2

A few ships still carry passengers across the Atlantic. Queen Mary 2, owned by the Cunard line, makes regular crossings which take seven days.

DID YOU KNOW?

The fastest crossing of the Atlantic by a passenger craft was that by the airplane Concorde, which did it in 2 hours 52 minutes.

Modern Safety

Thanks to safety improvements and new navigation technologies, it is rare for cruise ships to sink. However, accidents still occur. In 2012, the cruise ship *Costa Concordia* was wrecked off the coast of Italy. Thirty-two passengers died.

Human error is responsible for most disasters at sea today.

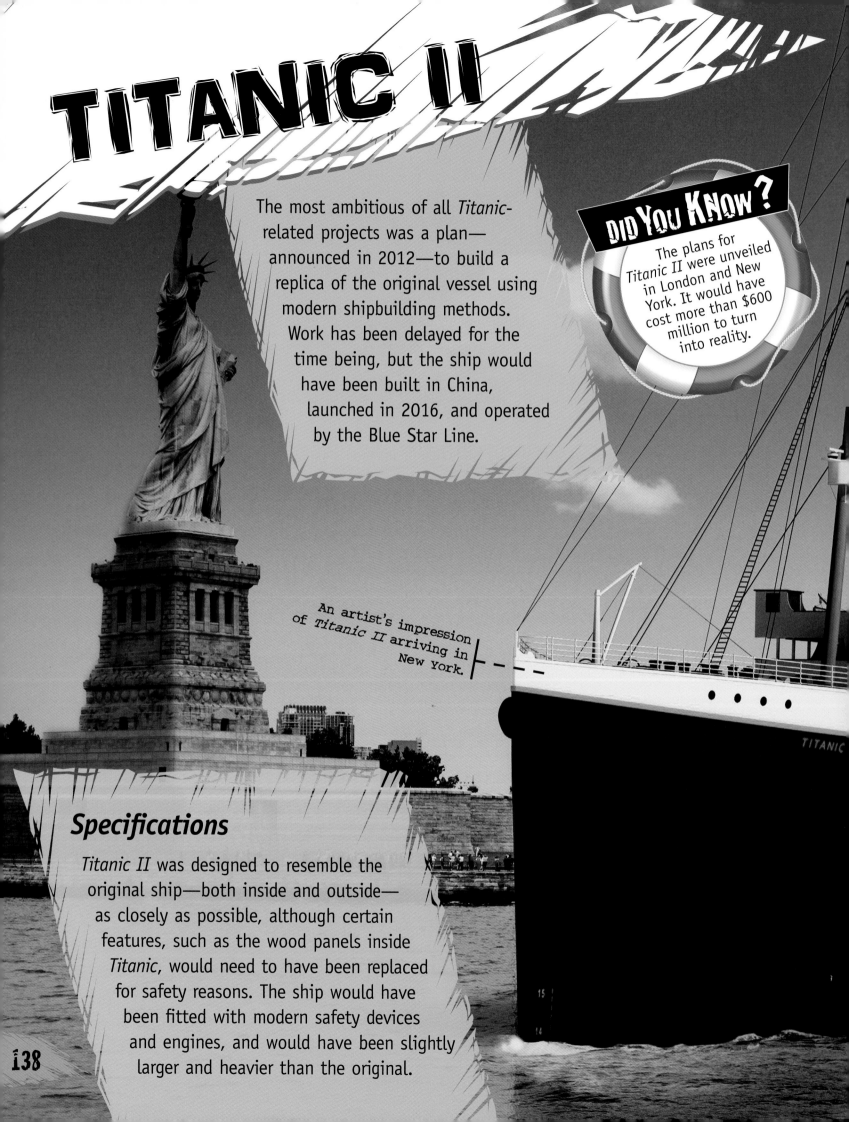

TITANIC II

The most ambitious of all *Titanic*-related projects was a plan—announced in 2012—to build a replica of the original vessel using modern shipbuilding methods. Work has been delayed for the time being, but the ship would have been built in China, launched in 2016, and operated by the Blue Star Line.

An artist's impression of *Titanic II* arriving in New York.

Specifications

Titanic II was designed to resemble the original ship—both inside and outside—as closely as possible, although certain features, such as the wood panels inside *Titanic*, would need to have been replaced for safety reasons. The ship would have been fitted with modern safety devices and engines, and would have been slightly larger and heavier than the original.

People

Titanic II was the brainchild of Clive Palmer, an Australian billionaire. The board of directors of the company to run *Titanic II* included Terry Ismay, a relative of White Star Line's chairman J. Bruce Ismay and Helen Benziger, the great-granddaughter of famous *Titanic* survivor Margaret "Molly" Brown. Financial problems meant that the project had to be postponed.

Benziger is related to Molly Brown, one of the most famous survivors.

Route

Titanic II would have sailed exactly the same route as its namesake, carrying passengers between Southampton, England, and New York. Work on the ship progressed beyond just blueprints—a 31-ft model of the vessel was made and tested. Contracts for the ship's design were agreed.

The design of *Titanic II* was very faithful to the original.

GLOSSARY

Boiler
A metal container in which water is heated and boiled to make steam under high pressure; the steam can then be used to drive an engine or a turbine.

Breadwinner
The member of a family who earns all or most of the family's income.

Bugle
A brass wind instrument which is blown like a trumpet. Bugles are often used to sound alarms or call people, especially in the armed forces.

Centenary
The 100th anniversary of an event; 2012 was the centenary of *Titanic's* sinking.

Draftsman
A person who makes drawings of buildings, structures, or machines.

Dry dock
A channel or basin next to the sea or river that can be flooded to float a boat, and then drained to leave the whole boat exposed for repairs.

Emigrant
A person leaving their country of origin for a better life elsewhere.

Glacier
A huge body of ice that forms on land, often in a valley. The glacier flows slowly downhill.

Horsepower
A unit to measure the power of an engine, originally compared to the power of a draft horse.

Hull
The part of a boat or ship that is watertight. Part of the hull is below the water, part above.

Hypothermia
A dangerous medical condition that happens when a person's body temperature falls to less than 95 °F. It can cause death within a very short period.

Knot
A unit used to measure the speed of ships and boats. A speed of one knot is just over one mile per hour.

Launch
The process in which a newly made boat or ship is floated onto the water. Launching big ships can be a complicated and dangerous task.

Maiden voyage
The first trip made by a boat, ship, or aircraft after it enters service.

Maneuverability
The ease or difficulty of steering a ship or other mode of transport.

Metallurgist
A scientist who specializes in the study of metals, studying how to extract them and make them into materials with useful properties.

Mural
A painting done on an interior or exterior wall rather than on a canvas.

Port
The left-hand side of a boat or a ship, when looking forward toward the front of the vessel.

Quintet
A group made up of five musicians.

Remotely operated vehicle (ROV)
An underwater vehicle that is steered and powered via cables that run to a ship on the surface.

Rivet
A metal bolt used to fasten together metal parts of a ship, bridge, or aircraft.

Senator
A member of the U.S. Senate—a group of people who meet to make the country's laws.

Sonar
Short for Sound Navigation and Ranging. It is a way of finding and making images of objects, often underwater, using sound waves.

Starboard
The right-hand side of a boat or a ship, when looking forward toward the front of the vessel.

Steam engine
A machine that can do work, such as moving an object or pumping water, by harnessing the energy held by pressurized steam.

Telegraph
A method of sending and receiving messages over long distances by using electrical signals.

Trio
A group made up of three musicians.

Tugboat
A small but very powerful boat that helps large ships move and navigate safely within harbors.

Turbine
A type of engine that converts the energy of moving liquid or gas (such as steam) into rotation.

Whitecap
The white foam formed on water as a wave breaks.

INDEX

INDEX